The Cat's Meow

BOOKS BY MAIA KINCAID, PH.D.

Animal Communicator Adventures: The Journey Begins!
(Formerly: *Being Human & Loving Life*)

Animal Communicator Adventures: Learning to Love!
(Formerly: *Learning to Love*)

Animal Communicator Adventures: Coming Home!
(Formerly: *The Joy of Being Human*)

Dogs Say the Darndest Things: Are You Listening?
An Animal Communicator's Dialogs with Dogs

The Cat's Meow: Chats with Cool Cats

Chat with a Cat and You'll Never Look Back

Wisdom of Love Publishing
P.O. Box 4761
Sedona, AZ 86340
www.wisdomoflovepublishing.com

The Cat's Meow

From America's Most Beloved Animal Communicator

Chats with Cool Cats

MAIA KINCAID, PH.D.

*For fellow humans who share
the amazing adventure of loving cats!*

*For Cats!
For your wisdom, love and patience!*

CONTENTS

You know how it is when you love your
pet and you can't keep your eyes off
him or her? Well that's the way it is for
me with my person. She is absolutely
precious and adorable! I could watch
her for hours and hours, and I do!

– Peaches the Cat

ACKNOWLEDGMENTS

To Cats of all sizes, shapes, and colors: thank you for being such amazing companions, teachers and friends. Thank you for standing so firmly in alignment with our human highest good, no matter what consequences you may pay to take that stand. Thank you for your patience, compassion and love for us humans!

I want to acknowledge my clients around the world for their generosity in sharing their dear selves and their precious pets with me over the years! I feel blessed every day for the delight I experience getting to know these extraordinary beings, humans and animals alike!

I want to also acknowledge my telepathic animal and plant communication students. You inspire me and bring a smile to my face through our fascinating and fun adventures together. Experiencing your work as you go out into the world is the fulfillment of my dreams of humanity awakening to its natural ability to hear animals, plants and the Earth itself.

To my dear friends near and far for the precious moments we share, you know who you are! And to those friends I see the most here in Sedona: Betty, Rob, Pat, Gary, Cynthia, Tracia, Debby, Philippa, Steve, Wib, Jane, Lynn, Olin, Ananda, Alexandra, Derek, Bonnie, Mariko, Reuel, Tim, Judy, Faith, Larry, Erin, Joanna, Sharon, Becca, Jana, Heather, Myra, Carl, Christina, Jeanne, Adryanna, Rob, Alika, Tara, Mike, Joanne, Debbie, Laura, Lynn, Rick, Kathy and Jay.

To Deborah Dobson for your excellent editing on our fifth

book together! It is a joy to work with you. I appreciate your friendship and your unending dedication to animals and Nature.

To Jane Perini with Thunder Mountain Design for the delight of having you as a friend and creative design partner, and the joy of creating book number five!

To my immediate family: Dev, Joyce, Bill, Tom, LaVonne, Joy, Dale, Lisa, Pat, Max, Chloe, Cameron, Jordan, Arianna, Lou, Amelia, Scott, Helen, DiAnn, Greg, Evan, David, Delight, Chanella, Kayto and Thai.

To Terry Conrad and his family from Dulles Media: thank you for your all your great work on my website and for your integrity and the delight to work with you and know you.

To Dev, my human companion in life: thank you for your endless love and support. You are an extraordinary human being! You're the best!

To my beloved animal companions: Delight, Chanella, Bart, Thai, Kayto, and Cookie for your friendship, love and ongoing mentorship.

To all the Colleagues and Comrades, (Delight's term for my animal friends), for your love, wisdom and inspiring ways, especially, Lemonade, Bint Cerise, Ed Mar Balek, Herman, Jule, Tigger, Tigger, Sugarman, Katie and Joey.

Thanks to the community of Sedona, Arizona for your warmth, love, creativity and inspiration, and to the Sedona International Film Festival crew for all the great films and fun events throughout the year.

To my dear friend Betty Tentschert. Thank you for being such an extraordinary woman. Your brilliance, your passion for life, your fire and your laughter inspire me always! You are the wise and loving force behind the creativity and fun in our community

ACKNOWLEDGMENTS

and I treasure our friendship, your laughter and your smiles.

Thanks to all the plants, animals, insects and to our Mother Earth for being our companions in life, and our inspiration, pressing us humans to expand and to awaken.

I wanted to talk with my Woman to straighten some things out in her mind, so I came up with a behavior that would get her attention. Simple, poop outside the box! Voila!

– Peaches the Cat

INTRODUCTION

I t is with great joy that we bring to you, at last: *The Cat's Meow: Chats with Cool Cats!* The pathway in creation of this book has been the most extraordinary adventure—a four-year journey into the mind, heart, and Spirit of the cat!

With the experience of having talked with thousands of cats since I began my Animal Communication career, I thought this book would come together easily and quickly. In truth, the co-writing of *The Cat's Meow*, with the cats as my teachers, took me to new depths and expansion in my awareness and listening abilities that challenged and stretched me tremendously. The word that comes to mind of which I probably learned most was surrender. Surrender any timeline I tried to construct to complete the book. Surrender to continually bring new levels of integrity to my life in preparation for their ongoing teachings. Most importantly— simply, SURRENDER to the teachings of the cats!

I am a new person from this experience! But wait! Let me share one other detail—two other, important details!

What began as a project to create a platform, a book, for cats to share their words and their wisdom, became two books. The books finally came together at the same time with the unexpected and unplanned adoption of two senior cats who arrived just in time to be sure the project was finally brought to completion. The second "Cat" book is called: *Chat with a Cat and You'll Never Look Back!*

I invite you to journey with me. Join me in these conversations. Make them your own! For you too can communicate with cats!

With love,
Maia Kincaid Ph.D.
February 2015

CHAPTER ONE

A Communicator's Journey

I t is a glorious, crisp Fall day, with vibrant blue skies and giant red rock outcroppings jutting out of this stunning, rich green and red valley! I'm in my hometown of Sedona, Arizona and here to share with you an incredible collection of conversations with cats that will forever transform your experience with them.

By journeying with me, you will awaken your own innate listening ability because what you hear will be affirmation of what you already know deep in your heart and soul. As you read, the pathways to listening will open for you and your love and appreciation for these extraordinary beings will grow even more as you experience who they really are, along with their dedication, love and tenacity to stand for our highest good as human beings. And, I must add, to get their point of view across, too!

You will experience smiles and tears of recognition and acknowledgment as you discover how deeply they care about us and how they fill our lives with love and knowing wisdom.

For the past eighteen years, I have had the great fortune to talk with thousands of cats from around the world. In my profession as an Animal and Nature Communication Specialist, I am very blessed to have conversations on a daily basis with many species of animals, plants, insects and even the Earth for my clients. In addition, I am active in developing and training new leaders in the fields of animal and Nature communication through my telepathic animal and Nature communication training programs; The Sedona International School for Animal Communication and Animal Communication University are dedicated to guiding fellow human beings in the awakening of their own innate ability to talk with animals, plants, insects and the Earth. I work with animal and Nature lovers, veterinarians who wish to add telepathic animal communication to their practices, children and young adults, agronomists, gardeners and growers of plant crops, animal trainers and especially with those who desire to work in the field as Animal and Nature Communication Specialists.

My days are filled with dynamic and fascinating conversations and classes with students both one-on-one and in small groups, via teleconference. In addition to working with students, I also work with clients, communicating with their pets and sometimes even with their children, husbands, wives, bosses and in-laws. Sometimes we may talk with pests in their homes, including insects and rodents, too. And when a conversation can bring wellness, understanding and harmony for a pet or a person, we might converse with organs, tissues or even cells.

In my work with students of all ages, they are lovingly guided in awakening their own natural abilities. It is such a joy to experience my students' discovery of their own listening ability and the aliveness they feel when they so easily and simply have their first conversation with a beloved pet. Even more precious to me is when one of my students assists another person with their pet or in awakening their natural animal communication ability. Throughout the years I have been doing this work, my life has literally been transformed. My conversations with animals and our neighbors in Nature have brought me peace, joy and fulfillment I never dreamed was possible. I was once a very shy person, insecure, self-conscious, judging and doubting myself, serious and afraid to share my point of view.

The truth was that I was uncomfortable being human, and not really sure if I even liked other people or being human.

Coming from being confused and conflicted, I am now a person who absolutely loves her life and who loves being human! I am confident and decisive. I found my own voice and I love expressing myself. I have a good sense of humor — I'm a comedian! I actually learned that from members of other species. I fell in love with my fellow humans and I really got the true nature of being human. Like I said, I love my life!

What was it that caused this huge transformation in my life? What comes to mind is that what I thought I heard as a little girl and a young person about the meaning and purpose of life from other humans never really made sense to me. It not only made little sense, but it wasn't something inspiring or interesting for me. It resonated with my spirit so minutely that for a time, I seriously considered whether I wanted to even be here or not. Because I was not very fond of the idea of becoming an adult, when I was ten years old, I distinctly remember taking an honest look at what I thought I knew of life and explored possible ways of terminating it so I could avoid what seemed like inevitable unhappiness in the future.

Meanwhile, the animals around me seemed to know so

much and for reasons unknown to me at the time, they were happy and peaceful. They seemed joyful simply in just being and were calm in the midst of our human dramas. My attention went to them with curiosity, as I pondered what they knew that made everything so good.

I had vowed to not let myself go past the age of 10. One day my teacher called home to say that I had never said a word at school, and now I was crying in front of the entire class. She was worried. My parents were concerned. I was at the end of my rope. Soon I would be turning 11.

I had been asking for a horse since I could talk and when my parents said we couldn't afford to have one, I asked them to save their money and not buy me anything else but a horse, even if it took ten years. I said I would rather wait. When they purchased me other gifts, I got upset with my parents and reminded them to please save their money. I had just about given up on them ever giving me a horse, but then my parents gave me Suzy for my eleventh birthday!

So, just when I was about to use one of the ways I'd learned of to depart, suddenly I had something I had dreamed of having my whole young life. (My parents say they don't know why but, "horse" was my first word as a baby.) Suzy-Q, a beautiful golden, copper-colored mare with a flaxen mane and tail was a dream come true. My life entirely shifted on that day of my eleventh birthday and what was looking like an ending became a new beginning. Despite how uncomfortable I was being here, I decided I had to stay and work it out somehow because I now had responsibilities and hope for the future.

My new focus in life was being supportive of my horse. Interestingly, she was one animal who, like me, was uncomfortable in the world of humans. My parents were newer to horses than I was and we soon found out she was wild and free spirited, and actually considered to be dangerous. But I loved her dearly and we had many amazing adventures together over the years. For many months, I was bucked off on a daily basis for even the slightest intrusion into our peaceful world. For instance, a fly would suddenly land on her hindquarters, a car would drive by, another horse would whinny and Suzy-Q was instantly bucking. Her antics would start a chain reaction of other horses at the barn where Suzy was boarded cutting loose too, along with young humans being taken to the hospital. It got to a point where other parents wouldn't let their children ride when I was there for fear that their horses might get spooked.

Amazingly, everyone was OK and somehow I never got hurt. I simply climbed back on and never stopped. My tenacity and laser-like focus to understand and listen to Suzy-Q resulted in me having success with her and being asked as a little girl to ride other challenging horses that no one else wanted to work with. I loved helping those horses find peacefulness and confidence while at the same time I was growing my own.

In time, my family had our own ranch in the middle of horse country in the back woods of central Florida. I was fifteen and already had a reputation of being an animal whisperer. People would drop off wild animals they found and animals they had difficulty with. A horse would arrive for me to work with, and a little while later the same day, my Mom would hear a horse trotting by the house and look out the window to see if one of our horses had gotten out. She would do a double take realizing that I was riding that same horse who had just been dropped off and who had either never been ridden or was considered to be difficult. Usually she would see me riding the horse bareback with just a halter and lead rope.

I loved taking an animal who was on the edge, barely tolerating their existence and have them confident and feeling good about themselves, shining proudly in their accomplishment for all to see. By the age of seventeen I had trained my first national champion, who went from being an unknown backyard horse to winning at the Arabian Horse National Championships in Kentucky. From these animals, I learned so much about being authentic. They were unique and dynamic individuals who inspired me to look for my true self and my unique expression. More than anything, they showed me the value of listening, and how listening in and of itself can be so transformative for animals as well as people.

In the midst of my work with "difficult" animals there were many wise, steady sages guiding me, too. For instance, our family cats, Cocoa and Mocha and our dogs, Winston and Witez. There was Bandit the raccoon, Babita the skunk and Quincy the ferret. There was Sylvester the blackbird and Ernie the gray-cheeked parakeet, and my dear friend and wise advisor, Bart the iguana. A little later came my horse Delight, who, thankfully, is still with me now and Chanella, my "princess" goat, Delight's companion.

Once I decided to stay, to live, I was able to bring into my life so many wonderful animals with whom I had rather automatic communication. For the most part, my communication with animals was seamless. It just happened so in some ways, I was actually unaware that it was even happening. Things just flowed and we were in step with one another.

There were a few times though, when I obviously was not listening and it resulted in some broken fingers. These sometimes painful incidences seemed like reminders to be attentive and to listen. It was as much about listening to myself as it was to the animal or other person.

I was beginning to look with curiosity at my communication and noticed that there was something going on there with myself and animals and people. I had memories of times when I simply *knew* something but did not know why. I think all of us have memories like this and I believe that each of us has the natural ability to know things and communicate intuitively too.

My father loves to remind me of a family trip we took when I was about 6 years old that resulted in a visit to a horse farm. While my parents and brother and sister stopped to meet the farm manager, I walked on, right down the barn isle passing numerous stalls until I stopped in front of a particular stall door. I was too short to look over the top of the door to even see if there was a horse in the stall. But I knew without looking there was a horse there, and that she was in trouble.

I went back to the manager, interrupting his conversation with my parents, and insisting that he come quickly and check on the horse. My father still recalls his astonishment that the horse actually was in serious trouble and that some sort of communication had obviously occurred between us, leading me right to her door.

As a teenager and young adult, I found myself searching and read books like "Think and Grow Rich", and "The Power of Positive Thinking" as well as books by Carlos Castenada. I was crazy about plants and animals and continued to be fascinated by the possibility of direct communication with them.

In the early eighties I moved to California with my family when I was twenty. I attended California Polytechnic College, studying Chemistry and Psychology and began to actively explore the western United States. In Jackson, Wyoming, I experienced my first real winter.

In the mid-eighties, I moved to Washington State and worked for the U.S. Forest Service. While in Washington, my horse Delight and I met and we were soon out exploring together in the Mount Baker Snoqualmie National Forest, traveling many a mountain trail, sleeping under starry night skies! While living in Washington State working for the U.S. Forest Service and volunteering for the local fire department, I completed an intensive herbal program in addition to a massage therapy program. Being in the realm of Nature, getting to know the plants and animals, while at the same time studying the physiology and inner workings of the human form were such amazing adventures—I will always treasure those years in the Northwest!

I was married in 1990 and divorced in 1991. My ex-husband was a wonderful man, but I just did not feel that our destinies were aligned in the long run.

Upon completion of my marriage and the massage program, in 1993 my horse Delight and I moved to New Mexico where I purchased an 80-acre ranch in a tiny village at seven thousand feet elevation. We had many adventures exploring the cattle country and Gila National Wilderness areas and lived for our year there without electricity. I remember riding Delight along some of the seven thousand five hundred foot mesas, and feeling like we were on top of the world.

I'd even ride Delight into town to pick up my mail and some supplies and, for a long time, some of the residents thought he was my only transportation. Café owners would bring him carrots to fuel our travels. Delight has always been powerful in getting treats wherever he goes!

A COMMUNICATOR'S JOURNEY

While living in New Mexico, I began my work toward a doctorate in Holistic Nutrition through a distance study program. Meanwhile, I worked with race horses who were transitioning to polo ponies and did some modeling for television commercials. I rode fence (repaired fences) on enormous ranches and checked and moved cattle, and worked in a café as a waitress. As a waitress, I remember people asking why I was there in this restaurant out in the middle of nowhere. Was I in a witness protection program or something? On the contrary, I was out in Nature as much as possible, listening to her wise and loving counsel and finding myself.

In 1994, Delight and I sold the ranch and moved to Bend, Oregon. While in Bend, I dedicated several years to my nutrition studies and completing my Ph.D. Many of my assignments were completed while sitting in a horse pasture with Delight grazing nearby, or in a high mountain camp with the Three Sisters Mountains looming in the distance, calling us out for an adventure!

As I completed my doctorate program in Holistic Nutrition, I found myself fascinated by the thought of how we nourish ourselves or not, by how we choose to think.

Knowing the power of our thoughts, I had a growing curiosity and interest in working with young people, and went to work as a counselor for teenagers hoping to make a difference.

Working back and forth in communication with humans and animals, I noticed more about communication itself, and I saw that there was a lot of automatic communication going on without my awareness. This prompted me to know more.

While living in Bend, I met some great new friends that ultimately led me to the discovery of my natural ability to communicate simply and directly with all beings of life. It happened one afternoon in the living room of my friends Dan and Carolyn's home. Dan had previously expressed his belief that I had some intuitive abilities and he offered to work with me. On this day, my first and last session with him, he told me he was having some challenges with his throat. He suggested I ask myself some questions of my own intuition to assist him with his throat. With his guidance, I asked the questions and immediately received information for him, which seemed to come from out of no-where.

Dan acknowledged with surprise—I already knew how to use my intuition - I just hadn't realized it.

That was the end of my lesson and a light bulb moment for me as I realized some possible applications for listening to my intuition. I could have much greater clarity and peace in my life. And, it occurred to me I could utilize this gift of intuition to communicate directly and simply with animals, too!

When I settled in to really listen to the animals and beings of Nature who guided me, what I began to hear from my conversations with them was sometimes shocking at first because it was so different from the way we as human beings see life. But as I repeatedly sat with their teachings, I soon realized to my surprise that their messages actually resonated with me in a deep way as being the truth for me. And, as I became more comfortable with this, I had a growing sense of ease and joy in living. I felt like I could simply relax and be myself. My own unique self-expression began to come forth and I was so delighted.

With all the information and loving support that I gathered in talking with animals, plants, bugs and the Earth, I received a wonderful gift in return—my true self, my purpose and my passion. I found my way home to myself through hearing them speak.

They helped me learn how to love being human, to discover the beauty and sweetness of our human species, and to love my life. For that I am forever grateful!

I'm grateful because as an Animal and Nature Communication Specialist, I get to experience transformative moments on a daily basis when I share information from a pet with their people, and when my students come alive in receiving information from animals.

Let me give you an example of a memorable conversation I had with a cat early on in my career about seventeen years ago.

It is amazing how someone will schedule an appointment simply hoping to find out why their cat is throwing up and what the cat would like to eat. But instead of getting this information, the person gets their life!

This particular cat shared the truth that it wasn't her, the cat, who had a digestive issue. It was in fact, the woman that lived with her who was actually having trouble "digesting" what she was experiencing in her life on a daily basis. The cat was merely giving her Woman another view of the tremendous stress and dread she experienced by going into work. In hearing her cat speak about the real impact her work had on her, and having seen her cat repeatedly throwing up and literally gagging, the woman was powerfully moved and realized just what her work really was for her.

Before our conversation, she had already tried all the suggestions of her veterinarian, who could find no logical reason for her cat to be vomiting so much.

The cat gave a short list of steps for her Woman to take to transform this situation and she took action right away. She acknowledged that she had put her heart and soul into her nurse's training only to discover that the particular path she had chosen was not at all what she wanted. She had been stuck for a period of time not knowing what to do, so not doing anything. But now, having really heard her cat, she immediately began looking for other options. Simply giving herself permission to explore new possibilities gave her an instant sense of relief and peacefulness. The cat's so-called digestive troubles, which had been going on for many months, ended immediately! And her Woman soon found a type of nursing that she really enjoyed. What this woman got from a short half hour conversation with her cat struck her powerfully as the truth, and transformed both her life and the cat's!

I will never forget how moved I was and still am by this woman and her cat, and what transpired through a simple conversation that occurred early in my career. These kinds of experiences are so miraculous, so frequent, and so much fun!

In 2009, with a tremendous amount of pressure from the Animal Kingdom, Family of Plants, the Association of Insects and the Earth, and, specifically from my horse friend and mentor, Delight, I published three books of extraordinary conversations I've had over the years with our neighbors in Nature on many topics of life and suggestions from them on being human (*Animal Communicator Adventures*). In February of 2010, I released my fourth book, a collection of amazing conversations with dogs called *Dogs Say the Darndest Things: Are You listening?*

Since 1997 when I began doing telepathic communication with animals professionally, I have been involved in a fascinating adventure with cats, awaiting the opportunity to one day shed light on their answers to our most common questions for them. I wanted to create an opportunity for cats to authentically express what they have on their minds and what they would so love for us to know. As you might imagine, it has been quite a remarkable journey adventuring with the Cat Kingdom!

Cats are wise and determined teachers. They can put us through a course of obstacles to find the truth and, in the midst of meandering, we find ourselves. It can be a challenging, rewarding and humorous journey along the way!

This morning, when I was out for a drive taking in a gorgeous sunny day, it occurred to me to ask the cats if I was complete. I posed the following question: Is there anything more I need to deal with or learn before releasing this book, a collection of amazing conversations with cats?

The answer I received was one I have long awaited and one I thought perhaps I would never receive. It was: "You are complete with your training at this time. You may proceed to release our teachings upon the world. People are ready to receive us in our full brilliance and wisdom at last. We are delighted! Good work, Woman!"

The funny thing that stands out in what they said is something I commonly see and hear with cats. Notice the words they used: "You are complete with your training at this time", the emphasis being on *at this time*, which means that my training with them is not over yet—of course not—but I can at least release the book now!

I must say that I had a few mixed feelings about this information, but when I thought about it, it made sense. Clearly, as long as I am talking with cats, my training will continue!

What fills me these days is gratitude and the desire for every human being to have the fulfilling experience of having a conversation with their pet, a beautiful wild animal or a favorite plant. I want everyone to know that this is absolutely possible and to have the opportunity to discover what is true for you and what has you truly being you, purposeful in your unique way of making a positive difference on the planet while absolutely loving who you are.

Secondly, I want animals, plants, insects and the Earth to have their voice! I cannot be the voice for all of them, so I am inviting you to join me! With you there listening too, they can have their voice!

Imagine a new adventure on Planet Earth where every living being experiences the preciousness of their unique expression and where we all, species-to-species, celebrate life *together!* Our fellow beings of life, including of course cats, say they are already there! They are simply waiting for us humans to come and join the party! WE ARE INVITED! LET'S GO!

CHAPTER TWO

A Different Drum

Most of my clients find me through hearing stories from their family and friends about how conversations with their pets have transformed situations that often seemed overwhelming and impossible to resolve.

We humans naturally want to help others. When we learn of someone who is having challenges, we tend to recommend what has been transformative for us. Sometimes clients of mine will go beyond simply sharing the idea to call for an animal communication consultation and they will actually purchase an animal communication consultation for someone they really care about.

It was about six or seven years ago when I received a call from Gloria. As soon as I heard her voice I smiled because she is such a precious and kind person — a beautiful human being! It is always a pleasure to connect with her and I am fortunate to have so many loving and extraordinary people to work with.

After we'd said our hellos, I gave Gloria the opportunity to share the purpose of her call. She began by telling me that she wanted to buy a consultation for her friend Janet. Gloria explained that Janet had never heard of animal communication before, nor was she aware of the clarity and peace of mind that an animal communication consultation can provide, especially when we have important questions for our pets. Imagine being able to ask your pet whatever comes to mind, in addition to any pressing questions. And, providing the pet the opportunity to share what they have longed to express—the thought of having a conversation like this alone can be satisfying!

Gloria wanted to let me know that Janet would probably call in the next day or so and I was not surprised when I received a call from Janet a few hours later.

Understandably, Janet seemed a little uncomfortable not knowing what to expect or if an animal communication session was worth her time and Gloria's money, but she had heard so much from Gloria and was strongly encouraged to call.

I took a few minutes to share about animal communication and how my consultations work. I let her know that our meeting would be over the phone and that it was not necessary for her to be right there with her cats—she could be anywhere at the time of our appointment. As I concluded sharing about animal communication, I asked Janet if she had any questions.

Janet began to speak and her voice cracked. I could tell she was doing what she could to hold back tears, and I felt for her. She asked me if I would talk with her cats. I could tell that she was having a tough time—I looked at my schedule to see where I could fit her in.

As it turned out just thirty minutes earlier I had a call from a client who needed to change his appointment to the next week, so a space had already opened up for Janet that same afternoon.

A DIFFERENT DRUM

When I called her a few hours later at the time of our appointment, I paused for a moment to give Janet the opportunity to share her specific concerns about her cats. But the first thing she shared was her emotional devastation at the separation and impending divorce with her husband. Apparently, he had left a few weeks earlier and she was there on her own trying to hold things together and hold onto the home, and meanwhile Susie, her 3-year-old red tabby cat had begun to use the house as her litter box.

Janet's other kitty, Sasha was a crème colored cat of Siamese and other origins. Sasha had been hiding under the bed for the past week and not acting herself at all. Janet was shattered from the recent breakup of her marriage and distraught with worry over the cats and the damaging behavior of Susie. Within a minute or so, Janet had shared everything she could think of and it seemed like there was a sense of relief when she suddenly came to silence. I asked Janet if there was anything else, she said there wasn't.

I settled in to have a conversation with her cats. I was on the phone with Janet and actually had never met the cats or her in person.

I asked Janet to give me a moment to connect with them. I began by saying hello to Susie in my head and instantly felt a wave of her personality overtake me.

When I said hello, it was like an invitation to join me and she did! She was a powerful personality and her expression of herself came like a storm that had been contained in a bottle and suddenly released. The force of her expression was surprising and startling at first like someone yelling at you out of the blue, but I instantly also felt her love and sweetness underneath. It was

31

clear that she was volatile right now and that her naturally sassy attitude and love of drama was unleashed with her anger!

She joined right with me, much like a person who is desperate to share their pain. With her dominant angry force, it was as if she overtook me and now I felt as if I was a cat. Not only was I a cat, but I was Susie! Although I was sitting in my chair in my office, I felt myself moving around restlessly as a cat. I felt Susie's style of movement much like I was inside her. But she was moving me with the force of her anger! I was moved by her restlessness—up out of my chair — pacing around the office.

Now mind you, remember that I was not there with Susie in the physical sense, I was at home in my office and I was on the phone with Janet. I was communicating with Susie telepathically and it is such a profound way of connecting that I literally had the experience of who she is.

I said hello to Susie again. This time she replied in a scream:

HELLO!!!

It was as if flames were coming out of her mouth, pushing her message; there was no question about her unhappiness with her current situation.

I said: Susie, what's going on? What would you like to say?

When asked a question, some pets like some people may take a moment to respond. Not Susie! Her response came seemingly before I finished asking her my question.

Susie yelled:

I'm angry! I have been abandoned! I have been betrayed! And, I don't know what to do other than to scream!

I felt compelled to know who Susie was angry with so I

asked: Susie, are you angry with Janet?

She screamed her reply:

I am angry with everyone! No, not really. We both were abandoned and betrayed.

And then she screamed as if she were having a tantrum:

I love him! He's my man and he has left me! I am heartbroken! I want to be with him!

Susie, I see how devastating this is for you. There is no question about the impact this is having on you.

Her anger seemed to diffuse a little bit. She paused for a moment and I took the opportunity to say a few words.

Susie, as you know, I am on the phone with Janet. Besides her own upset, she is really worried about you. Do you mind if I pause our conversation for a moment so I can check in with Janet real quick?

Susie instantly responded:

No, that's OK. Go ahead.

Thank you, I will be right back.

OK.

It had only been about 30 seconds of being with Susie and I already had a world of information from her about how she was doing and what she was dealing with, but I didn't want to leave Janet waiting for me in silence so I reached out to her and said: Janet, Susie is very angry and heartbroken. She says she has been abandoned and betrayed. She loves your husband and misses him terribly. She is not angry with you. She is angry with him and she is angry about the situation. Susie's way of expressing her anger right now is to make the house her litter box. She is very volatile!

Janet responded, saying:

Yes, I can see that! And it doesn't surprise me that Susie is so devastated with his leaving because she has always been his cat and favors him, whereas Sasha tends to be my cat and favors me.

Janet, give me a few moments with Susie again.

Let me talk with her about what she needs and see about getting her cooperation in dealing with this tremendous upset that you are both dealing with.

OK, Maia that sounds good.

I left Janet in silence on the phone for a moment while I moved my focus back to Susie and thought of a question to ask her.

Susie, do you know that Janet is really upset as well, and that she also feels abandoned and betrayed? And that she misses him terribly and loves him?

Susie suddenly responded with ease and openness:

It amazed me how quickly her energy had shifted from that intense rage to sweetness simply because she was able to express herself and be heard!

And, then she said:

Yes, I know this—we are both hurting!

Susie, would you be willing to work together with Janet to be supportive of one another in this challenging time?

Yes, I would.

Susie, do you have any ideas or suggestions, or requests for yourself and Janet?

I felt even more excitement and ease coming from Susie as

she quickly began to share.

*Yes, actually I do! Whatever Janet does to help herself feel
better will help me too! Right now it is hard to find anything
that makes us feel better but there must be something.*

And then Susie began to brainstorm ideas for Janet as if she
were thinking out loud and looking for some way to live with
and to heal the devastation she and Janet felt.

*Talking with her friends is good for her. Going for walks in
nature, sitting on a rock in the morning sun. These are all things
I suggest for Janet, and when she does these it will help me too.*

Then Susie began sharing ideas for herself in the same stream
of consciousness she shared ideas for Janet.

*For me it would be helpful if we play a lot. I love the fishing
pole with a string and a toy. Keeping me busy is good. Also, it
is best not to look at me and think how hard this must be on
me, or how sad I must be. Don't feel sorry for me! I know this is
coming from concern for me but it makes it worse. I can get over
this and move on. I am a strong cat, and I do have a life apart
from this relationship — just let me find it!*

I was enjoying Susie's openness and excitement. She had
completely shifted from being angry, and now was creating a new
life for herself and Janet! I wanted to encourage her to continue
so I asked her for more ideas.

What else would be helpful Susie?

*She (Janet) needs to be with me like she was before—just
normal and natural. Don't coddle me! My behavior is bad!*

*She has a reason to be upset with me and it is OK. I know she
loves me too. Ask her to stop being so hard on herself. It is hard
enough as it is!*

At that point I saw a powerful opening to get some specific
help with Susie's recent behavior of using the whole house as her
litter box.

Well, Susie, speaking of that, what can Janet do to support
you in using the litter box once again?

Susie remained open and her response to my question flowed
easily, with no resistance. She began to share suggestions for Janet
on how to put a stop to the house being used as a litter box.

*I encourage her (Janet) to think for herself and to make a
stand that she will not clean another mess of mine even if it
means I live in a small area. She needs to draw the line and say,
'Enough is enough!' She will feel really great in this and I will
love it too, believe it or not!*

Susie paused for a moment in her sharing, seemingly for
dramatic effect. While she was being so open, I wanted more
helpful details for Janet so I asked: What do you suggest specifically, Susie?

*I suggest that she let me be free in the house only when
she is there and can really watch me. If she sees me posturing
to pee or poop, she can use a squirt gun or squirt bottle and
squirt me with water If Janet is really consistent I won't have
the opportunity to make messes, and we can put an end to this
behavior that I know upsets her.*

She went on talking before I could ask her another question.

Otherwise, I can live in the laundry room with the litter box. Eventually, I know I will be back free in the house and using the box. But I cannot be trusted right now because I am so angry I could explode at any moment. If she will set up a structure that makes it practically impossible for me to make a mess, similar to how it is with a new kitten, this will help me express myself in healthier ways and will allow us to bond like we never have before. And we can do this right now, even in these tough times.

She paused again, so I began to speak: Thank you, Susie! I have a few additional questions to be sure I understand all of what you are saying.

Susie, this question is in reference to what you mentioned about knowing that your behavior is upsetting to Janet. This is a question many humans ask: Assuming my pet loves me, why would she purposely have a behavior that she knows causes me stress and upset?

This is especially confusing when a human happens to be stressed and upset already, as in the case of Janet. Sometimes humans even question the animal's love for them when they are feeling so stressed over the animals behavior.

Before I could say another word, Susie busted in and began to reply.

In my case, I love my Woman and when I think about it, I don't want to cause her stress but I am simply reacting to the situation. I am taking my anger out on everyone involved. I have given myself the liberty to be this way. And in the long run, I am pushing for my Woman to take an action that will be good for both of us.

She paused for a moment and I almost jumped in to ask another question, but she beat me to it!

Many animals will choose to exhibit a particular behavior to make a point to their humans. They clearly choose the behavior and are actually intent on leading the human to peacefulness and to feeling a sense of their own personal power. This is often the ultimate goal of the animal, even though it may seem they are breaking the human down by continuing with the upsetting behavior. We really love our humans and we want them to experience a kind of freedom and joy that is beyond what most humans can even imagine.

We also have great endurance and can perform beautifully in these kinds of unpleasant behaviors, for long periods if necessary. For instance, if the human fails to take a stand and take action on their own behalf, then the animal could seem to attempt to break them down because the animal continues the behavior and the human continues to go on as is and tolerate the unacceptable behavior.

What I am saying here is that we often purposely choose really, really unacceptable behaviors that REALLY push our point — especially us cats! We like to make our point unpleasantly and obnoxiously clear! This is not the normal way of communicating for you humans so it really hits you deeply, and on all sides too. It is flabbergasting to you! We seek to have you experiencing the simplicity of life and living authentically as your true self. Our behaviors and persistence serve to help you peel off the layers of falseness that you often unconsciously choose to wear.

In my particular case right now, I am back and forth

between crying sadly with a broken heart — I miss him and love him so much! Then in the next moment, I am so angry I could strangle him! I want to cause him harm for the pain we feel! Not really, I couldn't. But the point I want to make is that I am emotionally vulnerable and all over the place. I am simply being myself. I see my Woman dealing with exactly the same thoughts and feelings.

The thing that I see as my horrendous behavior is using the house as a litter box. It is awful but it also gives my Woman access to her own power and using that power to put something so unacceptable and seemingly so out of control into order. My horrendous behavior is a gift for her. She could tolerate it and accept it because I have a good reason to behave this way. Or, she could put a stop to it, bring order to the house and to both of our lives.

She could find her power and focus on transforming something right now in this vulnerable time. And, I can focus on my normal routine and find balance, comfort and feel good about myself by returning to the normal hygiene program.

Susie suddenly paused as though she were looking to see if there was anything else she wanted to say.

Then I had a thought, and I felt compelled to ask:

Susie, do you like Janet?

Of course, I love her! And we walk to a different drum; we dance to a different beat. He (the husband who left) and I were in sync with one another. We walked to the same drum, we danced to the same beat! We understood each other. He was my human, I was his cat!

*I love her (Janet), and I know she is the reliable one. She and
I will be together now. I want to go with him someday, but now
it is our journey! I love her and I do want to be her companion
and support her in our transition.*

Thank you, Susie. I am going to talk with Janet now.

Janet had been waiting quietly those few moments on the
phone while I was listening to Susie. I now shifted my focus back
to Janet, said hello, and shared with her my dialog with Susie.

After hearing what Susie had to say, Janet replied:

This is a relief! I have been feeling so horrible on my own
with the breakdown of my marriage, and so guilty and responsible for Susie and Sasha having to go through this — particularly
with Susie losing him too! I like the idea of putting in a structure
for Susie and also finding some joy for myself. And, I love that
what I do for me will help her find joy too! I also love that she is
OK about being my companion going into the future and coop-
erating in creating a new life for us. This is great!

Maia, can we talk with Sasha now?!

Yes, let me have a moment to be with her.

Hello Sasha, how are you?

Unlike Susie where there was a storm of a response, with

Sasha there was a silence and a hesitation.

In what seemed like endless silence she suddenly surprised me and said:

Who me?!

Yes, you Sasha! How are you? And what would you like to say?

I'm hanging in there! It's like I am down deep in a well or off in a cavern hiding out from the storms, wondering if anyone will ever notice me.

Well Sasha, we have and of course, you are important! Your Woman is quite concerned about you. How are you?

Well, I am actually concerned about her (Janet). I don't like to see her so sad and upset. I don't want her to hide it from me either. I would rather have her be authentic right here with me, but I am upset knowing she is upset anyway. I love her dearly and want her to be loved and fulfilled. That is what brings me joy.

Sasha suddenly turned her focus back to herself.

I am OK, I guess. I like peacefulness and joy and it is anything but that here at the moment. That is why I am hiding out.

Sasha, what about Susie, are you concerned about her as well?

Not really, she's a drama queen and she loves being on stage and having something to cry about.

I decided to ask Sasha about how she was doing with the man of the house having moved out a few weeks back.

Sasha do you miss him?

Yes, I do love him but he was not really here in the end and it was difficult then. It is rough now, but we can have a new beginning. I am holding a place of love and peace to remind them that this is possible and this is the path they will love.

When you say "them", who exactly are you referring to?

All of them, including him—I want them all to be fulfilled and joyful, authentically!

Do you have any suggestions or requests for your Woman, Susie or for him?

I have to admit that I like what Susie said about our Woman finding her joy and nurturing herself. This will help us all and this is the key to the gateway of a new life. I want her to keep going deeper and exploring, honoring, rewarding, and acknowledging herself — this will have us heading to new and joyous beginnings and developments, and the fulfillment of dreams.

Sasha, do you have any thoughts or visions or specific suggestions for them?

Yes, I envision a new sense of feeling accomplished and satisfied. And, I see a new sense of satisfaction in the simple joys of day-to-day life, feeling safe, secure and loved. This is what I envision for my family, including him.

As far as specific suggestions go, my biggest is forgiveness. She is beating herself up thinking she has failed. If only she had done this or hadn't done that. He is on the run trying to avoid thinking of us and acknowledging any harm he might have caused. He is trying to keep himself busy and engaged so he can forget. She, Susie, is a fiery demon of anger ready to pounce on anyone who comes across her path, hence my avoidance of her! I encourage her to remember that all of us are suffering in our own way and that the world does not necessarily revolve around her—and my request of her is to think about us too, and try to be kind and compassionate. That's really all. We can get through this and actually enjoy and benefit greatly from this stormy time, especially if we stay together, focusing on ourselves as a family unit. In this instance I am not referring to him because he is gone and I do not see him coming back. But the three of us can really thrive together.

Sasha came to a conclusion of her sharing. I felt grateful for the cat's ease and her stability with all they were dealing with.

Thank you, Sasha!

She quickly responded to my thanks.

Thank you, Woman!

I was curious to know if Susie was listening to Sasha's sharing, and if so, what Susie thought of Sasha's request for her to try to be kind and compassionate with Janet and her because they were hurting too.

Before I could state my question to Susie she began to respond to the thought in my head.

I heard her—and I do agree! I get it! I am being just like him! OK, I am going to make a promise to be more considerate of you, Sasha, and of Janet too!

She stopped abruptly and seemed to have nothing more to say, but I wanted to be sure so I asked her: Susie, do you have

43

anything more to say on this?

And, she quickly and sternly replied:

No!

I decided to move on.

Next, I began to talk with Janet again.

Janet, Sasha is doing fine really. She is the rock of your family, holding the space of love and joy to return to you and your home. I then shared all of what Sasha offered.

Janet suddenly seemed distinctly light and free in her sharing. She was almost giddy with relief from having held such concern and pressure. She excitedly began to speak.

Wow, Sasha is amazing! We are so close and it is good to know she thinks we can get through this and that she is helping. I like her suggestions too!

OK, Maia, well, I think I am ready to take some new actions and to begin a new life! Thank you so much! This has been invaluable!

Thank you, Janet! It has been a pleasure to meet you, Susie and Sasha!

I invited Janet to contact me again in the future if other questions came up or simply to share how she was doing. I never did hear back from her — not until I found her voice message on my phone nearly four years later.

I was checking messages in the morning as I arrived at my office. The first one was from Janet. I paused for a moment as the name seemed familiar and in her message she said she'd had a session with me three or four years ago. She said she had some questions for her cats with whom I had talked before. I called Janet and instantly remembered our earlier consultation in which I talked with Susie and Sasha.

Janet brought me up to date on her life since we'd talked. She had lost the home she and her husband had, and moved to a town near her family. She still had the two cats, and everything had been going quite well with them all, up until recently when Susie began to use the house as her litter box once again. In response to this, Janet had been in contact with her ex-husband who surprised her by saying he had just purchased a home right about the time Susie began going outside the box. He shared with Janet that he had wanted to come back for Susie all that time, but simply couldn't due to living arrangements that never seemed to allow for a cat. But now he could take her because he had just bought a home—the timing was perfect! He was excited to have Susie with him at last! Under the circumstances of Susie suddenly using the house as her litter box, and the fact that she and Sasha were fighting more and more frequently, Janet agreed to let her go.

Meanwhile, Janet, although still walking to a different drum, had grown quite fond of Susie and it broke her heart to let her go as much as she thought this was what the cat wanted all along.

Janet shared with me that the purpose of her call was to find out for sure what Susie wanted now and how she herself could be supportive of Susie, whatever that was.

So, once again like I had years ago, I asked Janet to excuse me for a moment while I put my attention to her cat Susie.

The same instant I put my attention to her, I was blown away once again by her powerful personality. There was no hiding how she was doing or what was on her mind!

Wow, did she feel alive and vibrant! I felt her sassy, bossy personality and her love of drama, but this time, she was full of joy. Being with her in this way caused a huge smile to form on my face. Her joy was contagious! I noticed too, that she was restless like she was when I talked with her years earlier. I felt a little unsettled being with her, but this restlessness was a happy, anxious kind of restlessness.

Before I could say hello to her, or even ask a question she began to speak.

I have been dreaming about being with him all these years, and I am so excited my day is finally coming!

I am happy for you Susie! It is so good to experience your joy and enthusiasm!

We dove right into a dialog like no time had passed and we were good friends. She responded excitedly right back to me.

Thank you! I feel so many things right now. I feel grateful to my Woman for her loving care, and her willingness to let me go to experience my life's dreams. I know it is hard for her to let me go, even though we don't walk to the beat of the same drum. We love each other anyway, and we succeeded in creating a good life together. I want her to feel good about what she is doing and to be kind to herself. She is amazing, I will always love her and she will always be my Woman!

I felt compelled to ask her some questions: Susie, do you have any concerns about going to be with your Man? Also, why do you want to go?

Susie took off sharing at length as I quietly listened.

I don't have any concerns. He is thrilled to have me coming back to be with him, and I know he will take good care of me.
I want to be with him to help him. I am a powerful cat/

woman, and I can guide and encourage and push him along to a joyful new adventure for himself. I have a powerful influence on him that he's not even really aware of. I have been working with him from afar to bring him to this place of readiness to have me there with him. He won't love all of our journey when we are together; I can be a tough teacher! And, I do not intend to make it easy for him! From the beginning he will have to earn my affections. I do not intend to simply love up to him—I intend to give him the cold shoulder for a bit. If he needs me to be close, I won't! When he relaxes and stops taking my aloofness personally, then I will move right in. It will be difficult for me because I want so much to be close to him, so I will have to be strong!

Please tell my Woman when he calls to say I don't like him and won't have anything to do with him that he needs to be patient. And, I don't want her to take me back! Leave me with him to do my work—I have waited so long for this!

I was beginning to wonder what this work she talked of was all about. So when she paused, I quickly asked: OK, Susie, what is your long-term vision for him, and what is it that you really want?

Before I could say another word, she had already begun to share her thoughts on the matter.

I really want him to find himself! I want him to discover how wonderful he is, but first he must discover his hurtful impact on others and how un-wonderful he is. I am eager for him to find his true self, but first he must remove the false trappings. I love him anyway but I believe he will be so fulfilled in knowing all of this. And, he has so much to give others that is not being given. He will love the opportunity and the gift of giving. I have many plans for him, and we have plenty of time!

Well, Susie, this all sounds great! What about Sasha? Will you miss her?

I will miss her some. She and I don't walk to the same drum either. She and my Woman, Janet, are aligned and in step with one another. Their relationship is a joy. It's peaceful for them, and there is no unpleasant drama. I think they will thrive together. And, we will continue to talk with one another about our humans because we can, just like you and I are talking now. I will be thrilled to be the only cat, and I know Sasha is going to love this too. With all my prodding and pushiness, she has learned to stand up for herself and we often fight. She is becoming quite an opponent and it isn't even her true way of being, but she is constantly defending and fighting for her space because I always push the limits! We are moving into a wonderful time!

When Susie paused in her sharing, I suddenly had another thought of something else to ask her about: I heard there is a small dog that you will be living with, and that your Man has a girlfriend. Do you have anything to say about that?

She responded freely and excitedly: Yes! I plan to warm up to the woman right away, and be aloof and distant with the man and the dog. Eventually, the dog and I will get along fine—I am eager to engage with the dog! But like I said, with my Man I will make him earn my affections, and I will make the dog earn my affections too. It will be challenging because I am eager to get close to both of them, but this is my strategy.

I was understandably curious as to why she had this differing strategy with the woman versus the dog and the man, so I asked: Susie, why do you have this aloof and distant strategy with the man and the dog, but not the woman?
Before I could say another word about it, she excitedly began to explain.

I have nothing to teach the woman, no work to do with her. But, I have everything to teach my Man, and a little bit to teach the dog.

That seemed to say it all for her, but to clarify for myself I said: And, what you wish to teach the man is what you talked about earlier?

Yes!

I realized that I had no idea what she might want to teach the dog so I asked: What is it you wish to teach the dog?

Oh, just a little about the power and wisdom of a cat! I simply want to bring her into step with MY pace of interaction and MY leadership in our relationship, nothing more!

To be sure I understood what Susie meant, I said: You mean basically, you want the dog to get that you are in control of the relationship between the two of you, and to heed and respect your wishes?

Her response came in a joyous blast, a celebration of words, and the unmistakable satisfaction of being understood!
She responded with undeniable joy:

Yes, that's it! Nothing more!

OK, Susie, I understand. Thank you for sharing and it has been fascinating to connect with you once again!

We were both all smiles and in a state of understanding and gratitude!

Susie responded with:

You are welcome and thank you for listening!

Susie and I were complete. Now I wanted to talk with Sasha to give her a chance to share so I said: Hello Sasha! How are you doing with all of these imminent changes?

Before I had a moment to entertain another thought, I heard her speaking with excitement and enthusiasm as I had not experienced with her before.

GREAT!!! I am so excited about finally having my Woman to myself! We are going to have so much fun and create an entirely new adventure together!

I found myself wondering how she felt about Susie leaving, so I asked her: Sasha, what about Susie, will you miss her?

Sasha responded right away, seemingly with great ease and clarity.

Yes, I will miss her some. We've known one another since our birth and we've been coexisting since then, but both of us want to be free to live our destiny. Mine is with my Woman, and hers is with our Man.

I noticed the way she phrased her last comment and asked: You still call him 'your' Man?

She quickly responded:

*Yes, of course! He will always be my Man! And, my Woman
will always be Susie's Woman too. We share!*

I felt a real sense of peace with her and I didn't have any other
questions for her so I said:

Good! Well, do you have anything more you would like to
share or any requests or suggestions for your family during this
time of transition?

Before I'd barely finished my question, she was enthusiastically talking again with determination to share on these topics.

*Yes, I definitely have my focus on my Woman and I want her
to be kind to herself because she is doing the right thing! She is
not abandoning Susie! Susie orchestrated this entire situation,
and it is finally being fulfilled.*

Now I had a question! When you say 'Susie orchestrated
this', what do you mean, Sasha?

*I mean that Susie has been working with him from afar to
guide him in creating a living situation where she could join
him, so she may really begin her work with him. There were
so many times where he was about to pull it off and create the
space, but then he lost his focus, stopped listening to her and
it was like starting over again. But she is very persistent and
patient, and finally he has followed through. Now it is important
that she stay with him!*

*Unknowingly, he has resisted her because she is a powerful
teacher, and it is not fun to be in class all the time! Keeping
her at a distance and having her living with us has kept his
responsibilities lower, and now he is in for some surprises and*

51

some opportunities to learn and grow quickly. Susie is intense! And we, my Woman and I, are eager for a break from this intensity and look forward to a bit more peace and relaxation. We could use that type of learning—some peace and relaxation for ourselves—this is our next chapter!

Now Sasha began to speak more seriously and in a way to be sure that I got her message and shared it with Janet.

I request that My Woman not take Susie back or even entertain it. Susie is his now and it is important for him to get that there is NO going back! If he thinks there is another option, he will spend time thinking about it and planning and will avoid his lessons. If he knows this is it, then he will have to settle in and go to work. Susie is a charmer, and she has been tugging at his heart all this time like a lost love. The reality of her aloofness and games may not be so pleasant, but I know he can get through this and thrive. She will help him in a big way. This is good for all of us! That's all I have to say. And for my Woman, it's: "Don't rescue him! Let him do this!"

Will you promise me that you will tell my Woman how important this is?!

Yes, Sasha! I promise I will tell her! Is there anything else you would like to say?

There was another moment of silence as if she was checking in with my being to be sure I was going to handle this correctly. And then she said:

That's it! I have nothing more to say.

Thank you, Sasha! It is a pleasure to be with you!

Likewise! Thank you, Woman!

I then filled Janet in on all the comments from Sasha and Susie, including their requests and cautions. Interestingly, the thing that really stood out for Janet was Sasha's concern about rescuing the Man by taking Susie back.

Wow—that is my habit! Boy, these cats really know me! This helps a lot because I was already thinking that if it didn't work out for them over there, I could always take Susie back. I also was concerned about how she would be with him initially and thought she might play some games and be aloof. She's amazing—what a character!

Janet paused for a moment and then said:

You know Maia, I think I now have a new opportunity to have even more peace and freedom from this relationship with him. Susie and Sasha have loved me, comforted me and now set me free to truly be myself. I feel so loved, and so grateful!

Well, I feel sad at the thought of her leaving but it feels so right. Thank you, Maia, and please thank Susie and Sasha for me.

I will, Janet!

I knew they were listening so I said: Sasha and Susie, did you hear that?

In unison they responded with joy and enthusiasm.

YES! Of course! THANK YOU, Woman (Janet)! WE love you!

And then Janet enthusiastically began to share about the new sense of freedom she was experiencing and how she now realized that she could simply do what she wanted with her life, including moving back to the town she had so loved and thrived in, but had left when her marriage ended.

She spoke with surprise at suddenly having this new freedom. I can do that now! There's no reason I couldn't do that now!!!

Her aliveness and enthusiasm were deeply moving. I felt some tears of joy well up in my eyes.

We thanked one another in what seemed like an embrace over the phone, and said goodbye.

CHAPTER THREE
Peaches

I t was a crisp fall day with bright blue skies! I suddenly found myself looking out the window, appreciating the magic of the suns light on the rugged red rock cliffs in the distance. I sat down for a few minutes to review my schedule for the remainder of the day. My next person to call was a woman from Illinois named Patty who mentioned in her appointment notes that she wanted me to talk with her cat, Peaches.

From what she wrote, I could tell that Peaches was very important to Patty. Her most pressing concern at the moment was that Peaches had stopped using her litter box.

Patty wanted to know why Peaches was suddenly now going outside the box and how to get her into the habit of using the litter box once again. She also was interested in knowing how Peaches was feeling and how she was doing with the kidney medicine prescribed by her doctor. She sought ways to enhance Peaches overall health and to find out why the cat spent so much time grooming herself. Patty thought that perhaps there was something Peaches was unhappy about.

My appointment was to begin in about 5 minutes so I decided to take a few minutes to get to know Peaches on my own before calling Patty. I said hello to the cat in my head.

Hello Peaches.

Hello Woman!

Peaches, do you know why I am contacting you today?

Of course!

How did you know?

I arranged it!

Really! I must say that this is not the first time I have heard this, and I also must admit that the first question that comes to mind is: How did you arrange an appointment between your human and myself?

It was easy! I wanted to talk with my Woman to straighten some things out in her mind, so I came up with a behavior that would get her attention. Simple, poop outside the box! Voila! Next, I started to pout a little bit. I love this kind of challenge because it really brings out my performing talents! There's a fine line between arranging a conversation verses a trip to the vet! If I found myself on the way to the doctor, I would know I needed more practice and that would be a drag!

In addition to my performing, just to be safe, I began to think about the possibility of having a conversation to share what's on my mind and how I am really feeling, and within hours I heard my Woman talking on the phone with her mother sharing my symptoms. *"She's pooping outside the box, and she looks so sad and concerned. Peaches doesn't seem like herself, but she doesn't necessarily seem ill either. I think she may be depressed and upset about our wedding."*

Next thing you know, Mom is eager to help her daughter. She suggests an animal communicator and sets out to find just the right one. That one was you and here we are! I'm feeling satisfied and really delighted with my performance. And now I am eager to begin!

Yes, you are! Well, now that you have me here listening, Peaches, what would you like to talk about?

Thank you! First, I must say that I adore my Woman! She is absolutely precious to me!

What makes you adore her so much Peaches?

Well. Hum... Gosh, now that you ask, it is tough to say one thing in particular. I adore everything about her! For instance when I look at her, I could watch her for hours. She is so entertaining, and so cute as you humans would say! You know how it is when you love your pet and you can't keep your eyes off him or her? Well that's the way it is for me with my person. She is absolutely precious and adorable! I could watch her for hours and hours, and I do! And I want her to be safe and cherished everywhere she goes. I also want her to have everything she ever needs and wants, including that I want her to be with people who cherish her like I do. I want her to feel fulfilled in her life and I want her to be freely expressive with her creativity and ideas. I want her to be in places where she is encouraged to be expressive. And more than anything, I want her to love her precious self like she loves me.

That is so beautiful, Peaches!

Thank you! That is what most of us "Pets" want for our people! You are our children. I want this for you, too!

Thank you, Peaches! Do you have any suggestions for your human as to how to have all that you wish for her?

Yes, I do! I have suggestions for you as well!

Great! I would honor your suggestions for us both!

For my Woman, she is on her path. She dreams of a lifestyle with a husband and kittens—children that is! And, maybe some kittens too! She dreams of being expressive, making a difference through art, and being a great mom. She has found the man. And, after a rigorous period of investigation, I finally approved him and now want to formally welcome him into our lives. Now that this part of her life is on track, it is time for my Woman— well, what remains to be prioritized and experienced is the expression of her creativity.

So, I hereby command my Woman to create a space in her schedule that gives her at least half an hour a day to express herself creatively. I request that she set up two different preparations. One is a creative station at home with supplies for painting, drawing and other arts, and for writing. In addition, I request that she create a portable kit that she may take with her anywhere, in case she is out and about at her creative time.

All time is her creative time, but she often does not create at all. What I am suggesting is that she develops a structure that has her actually creating art on a daily basis by having an appointment with creation itself. And that she also arrange to create at other times as well. Once she gets into this rhythm— once any one of you gets into this rhythm—you can maintain this fulfilling lifestyle throughout your life, and love it!

Next, what I would like to talk about is the guilt that my Woman and her fiancée are holding for me.

What do you mean by the guilt they are holding for you, Peaches?

Let me explain. She has guilt about being with him because it was just supposed to be the two of us—she and I. He has guilt about trying to separate her from me, or me from her. The bottom line is this: I am not in any way angry with her about bringing him into our lives. Really, I am not! I did put up a fuss at first and acted as though he did not exist. I also acted as though I was really, really angry with him being there. The key word here is "acted", because that is exactly what I did. I acted!

I am an actress! This is my work, and who I am. You could even say I am a drama queen if you like. And I must say, I am quite proud of my award-winning performances — they are believable — that is for sure!

The real truth is this: I knew at some point that I would be sharing my woman with a man. And I knew when I met him that this was the one.

How did you know these things, Peaches?

I knew it because I know my Woman. I know her dreams. I know what's important to her. I knew she would one day bring in a human for us to live with. I knew he was the one when I noticed how her heart opened up and she really took notice of him, and how important it was to her to get to know him. I knew she was the one for him when I noticed him shifting and opening himself to get to know her and to consider her point of view. Each of them stopped to notice the other and each of them opened themselves to consider new possibilities and new ideas. I saw this happening, and I knew. And I was happy about it. I also knew that he and I could have lots of fun together.

Each of them has felt guilt thinking I have been left out, thinking I think he does not love me. But I know the truth! And I knew it from the start—he was intimidated by me because he knew I knew her best. He competed with me and I loved the challenge because I knew I would always win. It was so much fun! Then he surrendered, and he knew we would all be together but he felt bad for competing with me and even requesting that I be given away at one point. Meanwhile, I was unaffected. But I acted as though it was the worst offense possible. I played it up big and they both felt horrible about how I was suffering in the midst of their joy.

Peaches, what was your purpose in all this acting?

My purpose was to really push them on their guilt. I sensed it and really pressed them to feel it fully so it was in their faces. Then they could take a good look at it and ultimately release it forever. I want them to give up the guilt fully because it is so damaging to their lives, and besides, it honestly serves no one and simply brings us all down. *The alternative is that we go on living together, everything seems great, but there's this nasty feeling in their hearts that continues to pain them unnecessarily forever. Leaving it like this is entirely unacceptable to me! I would rather they suffer a little now and clear it up altogether than to keep it just under the surface and have all sorts of other guilt attached to it, creating lie upon nasty lie!*

I am here now to snuff it out by playing ridiculous roles on television (our home stage) and have them experience this fully, and then be ready to release it once and for all. At this point, I already feel like my Woman is at the end of her rope. She is ready to let this go for good and to fully enjoy her new life with the three of us at last. He is not quite there yet.

Peaches, what needs to happen to help him be ready to let this go once and for all?

He needs to hear it from her! She, my Woman, needs to get up on the stage and tell him she truly and fully forgives him for initially wanting me to be out of their lives. I forgave him a long time ago because I knew he didn't know what he was doing anyway. And even if he thought he knew what he was doing, I would forgive him. She has tried to forgive him, but she has not fully forgiven him because she has not fully forgiven herself. I suggest that she forgive him, and she forgive herself, once and for all!

I am not the one with the problem! They are looking at me through THEIR eyes of guilt! All they need to do is genuinely forgive themselves, and then they can start off their marriage with a whole new beginning based purely on love, knowing that everyone, including and especially me, loves them and loves having them be together.

Peaches, please explain what they need to forgive themselves about.

OK. When they first got together, he asked her to find me another home. He had a particular viewpoint on this that made sense to him at the time, based on some other things he was dealing with. She refused to find me a home and in fact, considered breaking off their relationship over this. He came around and opened up to her point of view and in the process; he was able to really understand how much she loves me and how much I love her.

As he went through this he also fell in love with me, and I fell in love with him. Now we are all so close, but he still feels guilty for the time when he was pushing her to find me a new home. He looks at me and thinks to himself, "How could I have wanted her to be given away?!" And then, he feels bad about himself again.

And she has a sliver of doubt about him and a lack of trust with him over this important detail, which I overcame a long, long time ago. So, it is my request and my purpose to have them get complete and clear over this as soon as possible.

That all sounds really good, Peaches! I will share this with your Woman. Are you open to me asking some questions about a few other things your Woman was wondering about?

Yes, of course! I am open. And, let me guess.... She probably wants to ask me about . . . my health and pooping outside the box, right?!

Yes! You got it!

OK, my pooping outside the box is not due to some sort of illness—I will tell you that! The reason I am pooping outside the box has to do with my desire to have her call you, like I said. This habit is highly effective at getting some action taken by my humans. I will acknowledge that this behavior caused me to be granted an audience with you, and to get my words to her!

Really, there is nothing more to be said about the habit because it should disappear now that I have had a chance to express myself.

Peaches, what do you mean when you say the habit "should" disappear now that you have had a chance to express yourself?

It should! However, if she goes back on any promises she makes in this conversation or if she simply chooses to ignore what I have said, then the behavior could easily reappear.

OK, I get it! Thank you!

Secondly, I know she is concerned about my health.

Are you concerned about your health?

No, not really! I am happy as I am and I feel well enough.

Is there anything that would have you feeling better?

It would make me very happy if my humans dropped the habit of entertaining guilt. It's a downer in every way! Seriously, it is a drag to live with someone who feels guilty, especially when they feel guilty about us—their pets! Generally, there is no reason for it and it pains us to see our humans suffering, especially with something to do with us that is NOT true! If they gave up the guilt, that would make me very happy! And them too!

Speaking of the guilt, Peaches, being a human I know that guilt can be really challenging, and like you said, we tend to hang onto it forever. It becomes the backdrop of everything else we do. It literally lives there with us and is a filter through which we look at and experience ourselves, and our lives. I know it makes it so we are not fully expressed. It sounds great to let it go and simply not feel guilty anymore, but really, how can we do that? What are the actual steps or techniques that will have us successful in eliminating guilt once and for all, forever?!

Thank you! I am happy you asked that question because my Woman and my new Man need to know how to do this!

Let me say a few truths here! First, guilt is simply a habit of thinking. Let me repeat: GUILT IS SIMPLY A HABIT OF THINKING! It can be an addiction for some of you as well — no different than being addicted to a drug. Humans have to have their guilt fix! But habits can be eliminated altogether and the habit of guilt is easier to eliminate than some habits of drug use. That's the good news!

The bad news is that you humans tend to believe that what you think is The Truth. You think that if you think it, it is true. You give a lot of credit to the mind and believe that what it says is the absolute truth. And if it says you are a bad person and should be punished for finding your true love and bringing this person home to your cat, then you listen. And, despite your joy at being with your true love, you continue to beat yourself up about hurting your cat. Meanwhile, there is NO truth in what you are basing this on. It is entirely a fabrication of the mind to have you stay small — to keep you from fully celebrating your life and, God forbid, to keep you from making a fool of yourself! The bottom line is that this voice that wants to control you through guilt is the same voice that says, "Don't do any art, you don't have talent — you will be disappointed. Don't take that trip around the world. Even though it has been your dream forever, it's not a good idea with what's going on in the world right now. Don't go back to school, you are way too old and besides, you really don't care if you follow that dream anyway." The same voice that has us controlled by guilt is the same voice that wants you humans to sacrifice your joy and your dreams and literally your aliveness. Keep this in mind! Guilt is a fabrication of the mind! It is not true and there is no truth behind it. It serves no one!

The way to eliminate the habit of guilt is to notice each time you sense its presence. Call it out by acknowledging that you see it. In this case, when my Woman notices she is feeling guilty about having her man in her life she can simply say to the thought, "I heard what you said, thank you for sharing, but this is not true and I do not honor what you are sharing with any additional thought." Basically, she can acknowledge that she heard the guilty comment and even give thanks, but she is not going to honor it and believe it because it is not true. She may address it for merely a second and then move onto other thoughts, which she appreciates, approves of and agrees with. For instance, she can choose to have a lovely thought—she could think about how much she loves me. This alone can totally cause that guilty thought to fade away because it literally cannot survive in the face of the truth of her love for me!

Bottom line here, humans! YOU choose what you think about. Guilty thoughts breed guilty thoughts breed guilty thoughts, and before you know it, you have lost sight of what you are committed to. You no longer recognize your value, your voice and who you are as a unique living being on this planet.

Wow! That makes great sense!

Before you say or ask anything more, let me give you a few examples. You know how when you, what you humans term, "house train" a dog? Notice I say dog—we cats are not in need of training! Anyway, when you are in that house training mode, you do everything possible, including taking the dog out numerous times throughout the day and night and watching them closely, in order to avoid having them do their business in the house. You don't even want them to begin to have a thought about it, let alone an experience, because dogs who have been doing their business in the house tend to go on doing their business in the house. It becomes a habit! Similarly, don't let your mind even entertain guilt for a minute: Have your home and personal environment be guilt free, because the habit of guilty thinking causes tremendous pain and confusion to other humans, and especially to animals. Stop this painful habit now!

Do whatever you can to avoid dwelling in guilt. When you notice a guilty thought or you say something using guilt, correct it immediately like you would with the dog, and move on, staying in the guilt free zone. Be diligent, and have fun along the way and with the process. Don't do the classic, "Feeling guilty about feeling guilt"!

I do have a question, Peaches. You mentioned that guilt

causes more pain and confusion to other humans and especially
to animals. What do you mean by that?

*When a person has guilt, it lives in them as a belief, which
they hold as true. The person communicates and acts from this
belief. For instance with my Woman, she believes she let me
down when she met her man. So when she is with me, she is
with me with that lie. She feels guilty with respect to me and is
always apologizing and feeling bad. Basically, she truly believes
she let me down. As a result, I have to be with a guilty person.
It's like she's not even there with me because it is so ridiculous.
And I cannot reach her! I have not been able to reach her to get
her to stop this nonsense! It is no fun being with her like this! It's
not the way it was before and it is not because of the man being
here—it is because of what she is choosing to believe! That is
why I say guilt is a nasty habit and it creates pain for those who
must suffer with it, like us pets and people who are closest. We
lose our person to guilt like we lose a person to alcohol or drugs.
It is really no different! That is why I want it to stop now!*

I got it! Boy, that really hits home! Thank you, Peaches! And
I get why this really makes a difference with your health and the
health of our pets around the world. Guilt causes stress and it
causes upset and confusion!

*Yes! Thank you for listening! I know you get it now, and
I know you will share this important truth with my Woman! I
love her dearly and my Man too! I want them to have the most
tremendous life they can, and I want us animals on the planet
to have our voice, and to transform this nasty human habit once
and for all! I could go on and on!*

I would love to talk about this more and let's do this! But right now, we have your Woman waiting and I really want to share with her anything else that would benefit you health-wise and any other way.

OK, tell her the Chinese herbal formula has been helpful for my excessive habit of licking myself. I would also like a Chinese herbal formula as a tonic for my kidneys and urinary system. I want her to continue to be attentive to me and my needs, but also to keep in mind that I will let her know when I want something new. And I want her to keep a soft eye on me, anyway. What I mean by this is to avoid labeling me as having health issues and instead to simply manage my needs from a relaxed place of power. When she feels confused or uncertain, she should take no action. Have her check with herself regularly to see if she has some sort of guilt showing up. If so, clear it quickly and then simply acknowledge any other concerns. Be honest about them, then be willing to set them aside and simply be. She will know what to do! And she can talk with you again as well. In fact, I might request it at times.

That is all for me today!

Peaches why do you lick yourself so much?

I find it to be very relaxing and meditative. There's nothing really big going on here, it's simply something I enjoy.

OK Peaches, thank you! I am going to talk with her now, and do let me know how she does with the guilt.

I will! Thank you! And, let me know when you want to talk more! I have lots to share!

I will! Thank you, Peaches!

I called Patty right away.

Patty, I have been talking with Peaches—she is quite a character and she has so much to share!

She certainly is, Maia! I would love to hear what she has to say!

I shared Peaches message with Patty, and then there was a moment of silence before she suddenly spoke.

Maia! Wow! I just had to sit with this for a few moments. Sorry to leave you waiting!

No problem, Patty.

Wow, I really get what she said! This guilt has overtaken me and I am not the same person with her anymore. I am no fun for her to be with, and I also see how Brian is not fully himself with her either. I see how guilt is in the way of him really being his loving self with her. And, it is in the way of me being my loving self with her. When I am with her, I am thinking thoughts that I have let her down. I'm not really focused on her I'm focused on not being enough for her. It's like who is really with her is not me, it's a damaged me. I am coming from the desire to be everything for her but I hold myself as being a failure so when we are together she's with me feeling bad and being in my own head instead of simply being with her and enjoying. Now I really see how she is the one suffering here! My tendency when I am with her is to dive right in and start to berate myself for failing her by having Brian in our life, and I see that's the guilt again! Oh my gosh! I see what she's saying about it being much worse for her—I must stop this! I promise I will stop this habit! And I promise that I will share this with Brian. I promise we will both stop and instead simply be ourselves, and be with her, and start to celebrate our lives together! What a relief! Oh, this is so great!

Thank you, Maia!

Thank you, Patty. And thank you, Peaches! I am really touched by our conversation, and I feel grateful to you both!

A week later I said hello again to Peaches.

Hi Peaches!

Hello Woman!

Well, how are they doing?!

GREAT! I am so happy! And we are all having so much fun!!!

Fantastic, Peaches! Thank you!

Thank you, Woman!

CHAPTER FOUR
That Loving Feeling

When I said hello to him, I instantly felt a deep sense of relaxation that inspired me to yawn and settle into a peaceful meditative state.

He said hello back to me and for a moment he was attentive to my presence, but then in the pause of the silence between us, he drifted off to sleep.

I could have easily taken a nap given how relaxed I was but I had no time for a nap! I had only a few minutes to get to know this cat named Ben, and then it would be time to call my client, his person, Diana.

Ben!

Yes!

I thought I lost you there!

No, I am here. I'm just resting a little.

71

Oh, good! Do you know why I'm here, Ben?

Yes, of course! I called you actually!

Really! Tell me about that.

Well, let me say this. My woman has been worrying about me and it seems like no matter what I do to help her relax and stop worrying, she just keeps going. Notice for instance when you began to talk with me, you also began to relax and feel peaceful and sleepy. I try to do this with her and no matter how masterful I am at this, she continues to stay very alert and very concerned!

I get it—she loves me dearly and does not want to overlook anything with me. She wants me to have my every need or desire met with ease and swiftness.

I love her! I don't want her to worry though! I'm doing just fine and there is nothing really to be concerned about!

So, to get you to come into the picture, Maia—to get you to work with us—I went into the closet. It was the last resort for me. And, for my woman it was the thing that had her in an open space to listen, and then to call someone like you—someone who has confidence in communicating with animals.

That is very interesting Ben! How did she find me exactly? Were you a part of that?

Yes! What happened was I was looking for someone to help us, so I asked other cats I know in the neighborhood.

Are these cats you know personally from meeting them outside in the yard?

THAT LOVING FEELING

No, actually I live in the city and I don't go out anymore. I know these cats because they live nearby and I communicate with them telepathically. We all do this because it is a natural way to communicate. And, because of the circumstances of where we live, most of us don't have a way to get out and meet in person. We are very adept at communicating telepathically, so that is what I do! In my conversations with other cats, I asked for some assistance in finding someone to talk with my woman. I heard about you and then I began to work some magic to get my woman to meet this other woman to get the information so we could connect. I am very powerful and simply thinking of the meeting and about the possibility of my woman actually having a conversation with me to bring ease to her worries began to be a reality. Before you know it, my woman had the openness to seek help, and to take the information and go with it. That's how it worked!

Great! So, now that we are here, Ben, and we have this opportunity to communicate, will you share with me how you are doing?

Yes! Of course! My woman will say she called you because I began to live in the closet. Here's the deal: I am what you humans call a senior or geriatric cat. I don't necessarily like the terms, but I will use them here for the ease and success of our communication.

Thank you, Ben! What would be a successful communication for you? Why did you create this opportunity to communicate by going into the closet as you said?

THE CAT'S MEOW

Here's what happened. She was watching me with what seemed to me to be a microscopic viewpoint, or like watching me with a magnifying lens.

What can I say? I have been around for a long, long, long time! I am very distinguished and still handsome as ever but I am looking a bit ragged around the edges. I don't mind! I've had my day as a pretty boy, now I am a rugged looking man/cat! As you can tell, I have fun no matter what!

To go on, I needed a break from her extreme concern. So one day while I was walking around, I noticed the closet door slightly ajar and I went right on in. I instantly liked the darkness in there, I had a sense of privacy and I could see that this location would offer me the opportunity for a deep rest from my adoring fans, particularly my woman!

I didn't waste any time! I went right to creating a nice bed for myself deep in the closet, outside the main thoroughfare of the entry. It was perfect—no one could even see me in there!

Initially this caused some additional concern to my woman because she could not find me. She came home and her 19-year-old indoor cat was nowhere to be found. She looked and looked and called out to me. I heard her of course, but I remained hidden and comfortable. After a while, she happened to notice the closet door ajar and when she looked in she could not see me, nor could I see her. But I knew she was there in my space.

The next day, I came out to eat a little, but for the most part I have been living in my new hideout for a few weeks now. I love it!

OK, I know she has questions, and I did agree to cooperate so let's get to it!

Great! Actually, Ben, let me call her on the phone and introduce myself. Then, between the two of you, I can ask you questions and share with her until you both feel complete and understand each other. How does that sound?

Sounds really great—go right ahead—call her.

I would call Diana by telephone from my office in Sedona, and I had been talking with Ben telepathically. Ben and I did not need a phone; we could reach out to one another simply by saying hello. I just met him a few minutes earlier when I said hello to him in my head. Even though he lives in San Francisco and I have never met him in person, we could communicate with great ease. In fact, I already was quite taken with the guy and I looked forward to meeting his person! Diana had scheduled her appointment online so I had not met her previously and, through the notes she included in her appointment request, I only knew she wanted me to talk with her 19-year-old cat Ben, who was hanging out in the closet all of a sudden. She also wrote that she wanted to be sure she was doing everything she could for him because she loves him so much.

OK Ben, let me call Diana.

Hello Diana, it's Maia Kincaid! How are you?

Hi Maia! I am doing well. I'm a little nervous because I have never done this before, but my neighbor Janis, who recommended you, told me all about how you do your consultations and the tremendous difference it made for her and her cat Breezy when you talked with them.

My main concern is how Ben's behavior has shifted over the

last few weeks. He has some health issues we have been monitoring and he seemed to be doing pretty well. But then he started to hide out in the closet. He comes out to eat sometimes but that's it. We miss him and we worry that he's not feeling well. Is it possible for you to find out what's going on with him and how he's doing?

Yes, Diana, I can have a conversation with him much like having a conversation with you. And, I can ask him questions about anything you like. Let me say this—I actually have already met Ben. A few minutes before I called you, I said hello to him and I already have some information for you about why he's in the closet. Right now, I'd like to ask him more about how he's feeling. Let me have a moment with him Diana. I will be right back with you.

OK, Maia, go ahead.

Ben!

I'm here and I'm awake, don't worry!

Oh, good! Are you feeling well?

I'm feeling a little lazy and enjoying some quiet, peaceful time alone.

As far as your health goes, Ben, how are you really feeling?

I actually feel pretty good right now. My woman has this impression that I always have heaviness on my chest ever since the doctor found fluids surrounding my heart. In the times when I did have the fluid my heart felt swollen. When it was like that, it was like there was an irritation of the tissues and fluids flooded in to soothe them, but then there was too much fluid. My breathing would become heavy and labored. This concerned my woman greatly and now she has difficulty really shifting over to acknowledge and experience my good times—like now.

Right now my chest feels light and I feel at ease with my breathing. It feels good!

Otherwise, I do have a very slight irritation when I pee. It is another odd challenge that I sometimes experience. I believe that this too will pass in the next day or so.

And, other than that, I actually—well, I do have some soreness in my joints—mostly I have some stiffness when I get up and down. I move slowly sometimes and have to do some extra stretching.

You know, I actually have no complaints! I feel good!

Great Ben! This is good to hear! Let me share this with your person.

Diana?

Yes, Maia!

I talked with Ben. He acknowledged that he has had some fluids around his heart and lungs in the past and some urinary and kidney challenges and stiffness in his joints, muscles and tendons. However, he indicates that he is currently feeling well. He says he is breathing with ease and feels light in his chest. He is having a slight irritation when he pees, but he suspects this will be cleared up entirely in a few days. The only thing he does experience daily is the soreness upon rising.

Yes, Maia, he has been diagnosed and he is receiving treatment for congestive heart disease. He also has some kidney issues at times, and we have also been treating him for arthritis.

Thank you for sharing that, Diana. Let me check with him on a few other questions and in the meantime, think about what else you would like to ask him.

OK, sounds good, Maia.

Ben, is there anything you need or want? For instance, is there anything you need or want for pain, soreness, for your urinary system, your heart or lungs or anything else for your well-being?

Yes!

Please go ahead and share.

I want my woman to authentically share her fears when she notices them.

What do you mean by this, Ben? How do you suggest she be authentic and to whom?

I ask her to be authentic with her own dear self. That she really be aware of the depth of her fears of the loss of me, and her fears of the possibility of my suffering.

If she continually faces what she fears and simply takes some deep, slow breaths and is simply there with them, she will find that they actually pass rather quickly. And, in the absence of these fears, she will rediscover a sense of peacefulness that has been missing in her for quite a while now.

The peacefulness may only last a moment but it will be

nice. She will love it! Then, when the fear suddenly returns, she can stand and look at it once again. Be with it. Then the peacefulness will flood in once again. I encourage her to continue facing the fears. It will become easier and easier and she will be amazed at how peaceful she becomes.

The stress and confusion she is feeling around me is her fear of losing me, and fear that I am suffering or that I will suffer. Being in this state keeps her from really being with me. It has her feeling something other than herself and it has me feeling weird too! And, hence my desire to retreat to the closet!

I don't need or want anything—no new food, no change in my medications, no spe... actually, continue with the special treats! But seriously, what I request is that she finds her peacefulness and then she and I can continue to have fun. I am not going anywhere anytime soon. Let's have some fun!

This sounds great Ben, and thank you for the advice for Diana on dealing with her fears. I can actually put that to use right away for myself! I have a twenty-six-year old horse named Delight, who looks and acts like a three year old. He loves to be ridden and to adventure out on the trails. And yet, I have concerns about him overdoing it, so I hold back. I can see that being smart about things is important, but also really living is essential too. I can see I am holding him back by keeping him too sheltered.

I had the sudden urge to reach out to my horse to confirm this as being true for him and for us, so I asked.

Is that true, Delight?

Of course it is!

OK! Thank you Ben and thank you Delight!

Delight went on to say:

You are welcome! Thank you Ben! This will be transform-ative for our relationship! We appreciate what you have shared!

And, Ben replied:

Thank you both!

I was reminded of what valuable lessons can be learned in a moment of conversation! I know this will help me tremendously and I already feel a new sense of ease and freedom in my way of thinking about my horse, Delight.

After I'd had that refreshing thought, I wanted to get back to Diana.

I quickly shared with her Ben's request. As I was coming to a conclusion and before I could ask Diana if what I shared made sense to her and if she had any questions, I heard Ben telling me to ask Diana to promise him that she would really take to heart what he shared, and that she would take action to continually be with her fears when she notices them.

Diana, do you understand what Ben shared about fears and how to work with them?

Yes! It makes total sense and just hearing what you shared from Ben has me sighing with relief! I didn't realize how much tension I have been holding in my body and the racing thoughts going around my mind about Ben's health. I have been avoiding facing my fear of his death. I have actually been living in fear with him—no wonder he wanted to retreat to the closet! I have been no fun to be with! Wow! I really get it! I am going to celebrate our life together—we are going to have fun!

Great, Diana! Do you have any additional questions?

No, that's it! I am really excited about this! Thank you!

You are welcome Diana! Let me check with Ben to see if he has anything else to say.

Ben, do you have anything else to add?

I love this woman and I am so touched by her courage and compassion! I am grateful to you too! Thank you!

You are welcome, Ben! Thank you! You have made a difference for me! I plan to celebrate life with Delight too!

I said goodbye to them both and hung up the phone. I had a smile on my face and a warm feeling of gratitude in my chest.

About two months later, I noticed that Diana had scheduled another appointment. In her notes she expressed the desire for me to talk with Ben once again and see how he is doing.

Before making my call to Diana I thought I would briefly say hello to Ben.

Hello Ben!

Hello Woman!

How are you?!

Doing well! I have my issues sometimes, but they pass quickly, and then I am well again.

I am happy to hear that you are doing well, Ben! Will you tell me a little more about the issues?

Same as before—sometimes I have the fluids, sometimes the urinary, sometimes the soreness of my joints. Nothing lasts too long and like I said, I am really happy and feeling good!

I feel your joy, Ben! You seem light and carefree and filled with love!

I am! That totally fits! I am having fun!

Great! I got lost in feeling your joy and I actually need to call your woman now. I will be right back with you!

OK, I am here!

Hello Diana!

Hello Maia! You know, I want to tell you something. The last time we talked, Ben had been living in the closet for a few weeks. Well, later that day, after your conversation with him, he came out and he has never gone back in! I am really enjoying him and we are having fun again like we used to. It is such a relief and such a joy! Thank you for talking with him! I cannot begin to tell you how much you have helped us! I am so grateful!

You are so welcome Diana!

My reason for scheduling an appointment this time is to simply have you talk with him and see if there is anything he wants or needs now.

Excellent, I actually already began to talk with him. Let me have another moment with him. I will be right back Diana.

Thank you, Maia!

OK, Ben, let's see. That's right, you were telling me how you were feeling. Do you have any requests, anything you need or want?

I am reviewing my medicines, vitamins and treatments. Everything is benefiting me right now. I like my food too! And, my Woman is so amazing! We are having fun again! I LOVE to be with her! She is the most wonderful gift to me!
I don't have any requests right now. Life is good!!!

Great! I will share this with her.

Diana, Ben feels like a whole new cat! He says he feels full of love from you, and he is really enjoying interacting with you and what he calls his fans. He considers himself to be somewhat of a celebrity.

I heard Diana laughing.

That is so funny! He really is like a celebrity. I must say he has quite a following! Humans that is! And he is a gorgeous cat, even at 19 years old!

All three of us laughed!

OK, Diana, Ben does acknowledge the inconvenience of

sometimes having fluids and heaviness around the heart, but he says it is nothing like it was before. Now it is a hint of the past and it alerts him to keep abreast of it. Similarly, he has the possibility of experiencing some kidney/urinary challenges but they too are a tiny fraction of the experience he had before, and they too are short lived. He acknowledges that his health could shift at anytime but he is happy and doing exactly what he wants to do. And, he likes the team of experts you have working with you for his well-being. He also likes the program you currently have him on. He indicates that he would not change any of the dosages at all.

That's great Maia! He seems to be doing really well from what I see here too. He is active. He's engaging with us, and his fans too! And, he is out with us all the time like he always was in the past, other than his stint in the closet!

Diana, what you shared matches what he is sharing with me, and what I am experiencing being with him. His joy is contagious! I want to acknowledge you, Diana, for your openness to really listen to what Ben shared with you the last time we talked. Your willingness to take action on your cat's requests, right away, had you bravely facing your fears of losing him. And, by facing your fears, you rediscovered the peacefulness and love you once celebrated with Ben. You brought back that loving feeling between the two of you!

I am inspired! And, I feel grateful to have experienced this with the two of you! Thank you, Diana, and thank you Ben!

Before Diana could say a word, Ben jumped in and said:

Thank you, Woman! (to me)

THAT LOVING FEELING

I was moved to tears.

And then Diana said:

Maia, I don't know what to say. I appreciate you so much!

CHAPTER FIVE

Lance

I t's tough to talk about a Sedona morning without saying something about the magical beauty of this location on
Earth! As I left my driveway heading southwest, my eyes
were drawn toward the enormous rock outcropping we locals
call "Thunder Mountain" which seemed to mysteriously and dra-
matically rise up out of the valley floor. The sun was glinting on
Coffee Pot Rock at the northeastern end of Thunder Mountain as
I made my way onto highway 89A. I was on my way out to the
barn to see my 28-year-old horse, mentor, and friend, Delight,
and his companion goat, Chanella.

Delight is a small horse, a pinto pony with four white socks
and a dark brown coat with white splashes of color on his legs,
back and hindquarters. Although he is not large in stature, he's
a powerful, athletic horse, often mistaken for a mustang because
of his joy in being free to run, and his wise and solid presence.
Delight loves to be ridden and very much enjoys walks in the Red
Rocks too! Chanella, his friend, is an adorable ginger colored goat

with a tiny faint white star between her long, floppy ears. Because of her ginger color, her white markings don't stand out very much.

Before going to the barn I planned to stop at a friend's home to pick up a remedy for Chanella, who had injured some tendons in her right hind leg. The veterinarian had already been out and he bandaged her from her thigh all the way down to her cloven hooves to keep her leg immobilized so the tendons could heal. I wanted to do everything possible to assist my sweet goat in healing her leg.

We have wonderful resources in Sedona and my friend Jane is one of the best! She is a homeopathic practitioner who puts together remedies for both humans and animals. I pulled into her driveway and walked up to the front door and as I stood back waiting for Jane, a cat suddenly appeared on the front step. He had a stripped grey coat with short hair that looked soft as velvet. He was of medium height with a lean form, and I guessed him to be around a year old. It appeared that he too, was waiting for Jane. Suddenly the door opened and before I could say hello to either the cat or Jane, he moved passed me into the house with great confidence, as if he had lived there since his birth. This surprised and intrigued me because I had just seen Jane a few days earlier and she did not have a cat then! As he walked, I noticed he was a little thin and moved with a slight stiffness in his left hip, but otherwise looked healthy. He let me know that it was OK for me to be there and welcomed me to follow him in. I was amused!

As Jane stepped back from the doorway and invited me in, she noticed my puzzled look. Without having to ask me what I was puzzled about she explained that the cat had simply showed up at her door a few days prior and now acted as if he owned the place. Jane began to talk quickly and excitedly about her experience with him, and it was obvious that she had some concerns about him. She thought he was too thin and was trying to find something he would eat. She asked if I would talk with him while I was there so I sat down in her living room to hear more about her questions and what she was experiencing with the cat.

Jane's biggest concern at the moment was finding something he would eat in the hope that he would gain weight. The first day the cat arrived, she went out to the local market to get a few cans of cat food. When she opened a can of food and put it out for him to eat, he went to the dish right away as if he was hungry, but simply sniffed it, paused for a moment, and then walked away. Then she opened another can of cat food and gave him some of that. He ate a few bites. The next thing she knew, she was out shopping again, returning with numerous little cans of the finest cat foods she could find, hoping to find a flavor or type of food he would eat. She opened one can of cat food after another and he sniffed each one, and simply walked away. Finally, she had all ten cans of cat food lined up across the kitchen floor; he had sniffed each of them, did not eat a bite, and was sitting nearby surveying the buffet. She was frustrated and worried about him not eating.

When Jane finished sharing I took the opportunity to say, "Jane, let me ask the cat a few questions." Clearly relieved, she replied, " Good!"

As Jane and I sat comfortably in the living room, I took a moment to turn my attention to the cat, who had now moved off to another room in the house.

When I meet an animal or a person, I like to remember to

simply make myself available to listen. We live in a world where being heard is a marvelous and rare thing. We often tune people out because we think we have already heard what they said or what they are going to say, especially those who are closest to us.

But when we do this, we usually fail to hear what they are really talking about, what their true concerns are and what they so want to share. Through my listening experiences with people and pets, I have discovered that the simple act of listening can have a profound and transformative effect on both the speaker and the listener.

I spent a few moments listening to Jane and now while I sat there quietly in the living room with her, I began to focus on the cat, who was still off in another area of the house.

I simply thought of him and said hello to him silently in my head.

My focus on him immediately caused a smile to form quickly on my face. It was no longer simply me; I was now experiencing another living being with a distinct personality and energy all his own. His personality characteristics and way of being in the world were very different than what I generally experience myself. The first thing I noticed, and what generated a natural smile on my face, was his rather flamboyant nature. He reminded me of a rather cocky teenager. It was hard not to like him and I must say that I was quite impressed with his confidence and how, though he had only arrived a few days prior, he'd instantly found his best sleeping places, had a woman eagerly looking to please him and he was now questioning me to find out who I was and why I was at the house. It still amazed me that three days ago when I was visiting Jane, this cat was not even in her life and so much had changed in such a short amount of time. But it wasn't as if he was "her" cat—it was as if she was his human! And, he was not eager to share her with just anyone!

Underneath all the outward flamboyance, he shared that he was delighted to be there and had never had it so good!

I had taken time to simply get to know him and allow him to share, and now it was time to ask him some specific questions. I wanted to get some answers for Jane about the food, and also thought it would be interesting to know where he came from and why he was here now. And I wanted to simply listen to whatever he wanted to say.

While still sitting there with Jane, with no cat in sight, I began to have a dialog with him in my head. Unbeknownst to her I began to carry on a conversation with the cat as she and I sat there in silence. It began like this:

I said, Hello, Cat. And he replied:

Hello, Human.

He had a way of speaking that belied a know-it-all, bossy attitude. It landed for me as a silly, lighthearted attempt at being tough and cool, but I could tell he didn't take himself too seriously—I liked his sense of humor right off!

I decided to ask him a question: Do you know that Jane is concerned about you having the nutrition you need?

Yes, of course!

Also, do you understand that she is confused by your behavior of walking away from the food and that she is frustrated because it seems you don't like any of the food she provides? She doesn't know what else to do.

To this the cat quickly responded:

Yes, I know all that!

And then I asked him: What would you like to eat?

Don't worry! I will eat when I want to. I like the variety she provides and I would like to continue having choices like this.

Cat, are you saying that you are not that hungry?

Yes, that's what I am saying. When I am hungry I will eat, but I would like her to continue giving me many choices. I like that!

So, basically, you would like Jane to continue putting out the buffet, and when you are hungry, you will eat what you like.

YES!

OK, I think I understand what you are saying.

Jane looked over at me at that moment because she saw the smile on my face grow and she asked, "What's going on Maia?" I said, "The cat wants you to keep putting out the buffet—he likes it! And he says he will eat when he's hungry. Don't worry!" To which Jane replied, "Great—well, that's not going to work!" Then she shared a flurry of other questions and concerns. "Also, my second question beyond the food was, where does he live? Does he have a home? Why is he here? And is he OK? And, ultimately I am wondering how I can find him a good home if he needs one, because I am not set up to have a cat right now."

I responded, "Let me ask him those questions. But first, with regard to the food, you can simply give him one choice each day and notice what he likes and doesn't—he will tell you. He prefers to have the buffet but I know this simply does not work."

And then I made a comment to the cat: As much as you like this buffet of choices, Cat, it's not really necessary, is it? He made a quick, yet reluctant response.

No.

Then I decided to jump right into a dialog with him by asking more questions. Cat, where did you come from? What brings you to Jane's and is there anything you need or want?

But our conversation came to an abrupt halt. There was a sudden hesitation on his part, and it seemed there was even some resistance to respond. In the silence that followed, I found myself thinking of the intrigue and mystery of the day-to-day life of an action hero, complete with music and all the ensuing drama. I sensed that the cat held himself in this kind of mystique and that revealing his true-life day-to-day adventures could shift everything for him. I understood, yet I thought it important to know something about his life before he arrived at Jane's house a few days ago and why he was here now. So I encouraged him to simply share with us the basics and what he was comfortable with us knowing.

Cat, I understand you don't want to reveal every detail of your life, but would you be willing to share with us a little bit about yourself so we can understand why you are here and what you want?

Before I could think or say another thing, the silence was over as quickly as it came upon us, and he began to speak freely about his life.

I used to live in a neighborhood not far from here. I liked my home all right, but it wasn't all I wanted it to be. I wasn't noticed much and could be gone for days on an adventure, and no one would even wonder where I had gone. It was kind of like it was OK for me to be there but it wasn't that important— like they really didn't care about me that much. So, I created a wonderful world of adventure exploring around the house and nearby homes. I dreamed of having a human who would value my presence and want to talk with me. I will admit I like to entertain, and I like being the center of attention.

Then he suddenly began to talk about Jane's home.

I had been watching this home for a while.

Cat, what do you mean by "watching"?

I would be nearby and notice the energy emanating from the home.

Cat, sorry to ask so many questions, but I really want to understand what you mean by "the energy emanating from the house", and I know Jane will find this interesting too.

Well, I can look at homes with my eyes and with my heart. I know you will want to know more! What I mean by this is that I may look over at a home with my eyes in the normal physical sense. And, I may look at it with the focus of my heart going there as well. Simply said, when my eyes are focused in that direction, I ask my heart to focus there too, just like my heart is a set of eyes. When you do this you will feel yourself engage in a new way. This is fairly automatic for us Cats, us animals as well, I suppose.

94

Anyway, I was engaging in this way on one occasion and noticed a wonderful warm, welcoming feeling coming from this home. I was looking from my youth and innocence and I was met by love, compassion and kindness. I instantly felt welcome and I knew this was my home! I trotted right on over and much to my surprise, the door happened to open just as I arrived and just as someone else was leaving the house. I ran right in, to the amazement of the humans standing there. My newly chosen woman calmly and amusedly went back into her house and searched until she found me snooping around the kitchen. I was sniffing the floors and lower cabinets for food, and then of course I jumped up on the counter to see what I could find there. When she saw me doing that, she looked around and found me some cat food from her last cat and I had a little snack. Then I wandered about the house peacefully until I found just the right spot to take my nap.

I found the home of my dreams, and now I have a woman who loves me!

I suddenly had a sad thought and a sinking feeling in my heart. I needed to be sure this cat knew where Jane stood on the issue of having a cat. Before I could gather my thoughts any further, I found myself simply telling the cat what was on my mind.

Cat, do you realize that Jane doesn't see herself as a suitable person for you at this time?

I know, I know. And, I'm not worried at all. We'll work it all out, I can assure you!

I was totally surprised by his genuine lack of concern. I felt no

concern whatsoever in his communication, and I felt no concern
in his being either. I was concerned, but he wasn't! I didn't know
what else to say or ask on this topic so I decided to ask him some
other questions.

OK, let me ask you one additional thing and then we can
look into this living situation a little bit more. Cat, how is your
health?

*I am healthy! I do have an old injury that I am still healing.
It is my leg and hip, which I damaged in an incident with a door
and a human. I still have some soreness at times and sometimes
I walk a little funny, but really, it is no big deal. And it is healing
well.*

Is there anything you need or want for your leg and hip, or
any other requests?

*My New Woman has some remedies to help me with my leg
and hip, and also she has some remedies that will help me settle
in here. She knows exactly what to give me.*

Suddenly, I was drawing a blank on what else I could ask
him. We were back to the topic of his long-term living situation,
back to the question I wanted to avoid!

So I simply asked him: Cat, what do you intend to do, and
what do you suggest for Jane? To which he quickly and know-
ingly responded.

*I intend to stay here at her side and soak up all the love she
has to give to heal my wounds and fortify my heart. Then I plan
to settle in even more and enjoy my life here with her and to*

share my love with her.

I decided to ask the next obvious question: Cat, what if she continues to insist that she is not the one and you must live elsewhere? To which he replied confidently and without hesitation:

I will continue to be patient with her until she comes around and realizes that she is thrilled to have me here with her!

At this point, Jane interrupted my conversation with the cat to ask what I was hearing from him. I shared quickly and matter-of-factly about his past injury, how it was healing, that she would know which homeopathic remedies would help him, as well as his plans to stay forever and be her cat, until she surrendered, no matter what.

The last words landed as a surprise and the three of us fell into a moment of silence, which ended suddenly and finally with a big sigh from Jane, and a quiet moment of knowing clarity—the kind of knowing without question in our minds and hearts what was destined for their future. There was a new sense of peacefulness and surrender.

I thanked the cat for our conversation and for the inspiration he was in seeing something he wanted for himself and really going after it.

Thank you, Woman! You have been influential in the fulfillment of my dreams to be with this woman and create a new life for myself.

You are welcome, Cat!

At this point, I acknowledged Jane for having such an enormous heart to take Cat in and to consider a shift in her life to include Cat as her friend and responsibility, particularly when she was not thinking it was the best time for her.

Now it was time to focus on my original reason for visiting Jane that day—to find help for my goat Chanella in the form of a homeopathic remedy to assist her in healing her injured leg. As it turned out, Chanella responded very well and she was soon getting around with ease and even her old gracefulness. Jane made a difference with her remedies.

It was a few months later when I saw Jane again. This time I went to her house to meet with a small group of friends to share about our projects and be of support to each other in what we were creating. When I came into the house I instantly spotted Cat, who was resting quietly on the couch next to Jane as she worked on the final elements of her new book. Jane had named him Lance and he had become a wonderful companion and a joy to her. I asked Lance how things were going for him.

Lance, how do you like your new life?

I LOVE it! I LOVE my Woman! This is a dream come true!

I smiled, seeing the joy between Jane and Lance!

It was a few more months before I saw Jane and Lance again. This time I was at Jane's home office to pick up another remedy for Chanella, who was doing well, getting out and moving around on her leg more each day. We wanted to continue to offer her support though the remedy Jane prepared.

When I arrived, Lance was hanging around the door and he walked into the office with me at his side. Seeing that I was interacting with the cat, Jane shared how they were doing. "He's not as companionable now. When I go to pick him up and give him some love, he walks off. He doesn't sit with me like he did before. I am a little disappointed in the way he is being after having such a nice time of togetherness in the beginning. I don't know if he even likes me anymore. In fact, he reminds me of some of the men I have dated who can be so kind and attentive at first, and then seem like they are off in a different world."

Feeling her disappointment and sense of loss after having such a wonderful time of closeness, I suggested I check in with him to see how he was doing and to see what he had to say about his seeming aloofness.

Before I could formulate a question in my mind, Lance began to eagerly share with me.

I absolutely ADORE her! It is amazing to me that she thinks I don't like her anymore! Sometimes I play games with her. When I know she wants me close, I will act like I don't want to be close. Sometimes I walk away or face another direction or act restless like I don't want to be held. She takes it personally and thinks I don't like her. I am just playing! I want her to really get that no matter what I am doing or not doing, I ADORE her! There is no way I can think of her any other way—that is simply the way it is. When she gets this, I won't need to play this silly game anymore and I won't want to! I will have to be really close—I won't be able to stay away from her.

She thinks I am pushing her away, but she is really pushing me away! She starts to think of herself in a judgmental way and she thinks that she is not worthy of my love. When she is like this, I can do nothing other than to be distant. She won't let me in because that is her reality. But she thinks it's me, not her! When she loves herself and is open—truly open—to receive love, I will be there close! She will realize that she is loved no matter how I am with her in the moment.

As long as she determines her own lovability by what I do or don't do, I cannot be close. It is my dream for her to know how precious she is, and to simply know that, without being dependent on me.

We have come to a place in our relationship where we can go even deeper with our love. We can have even more joy and we will get there—I am not worried!

Thank you for asking Woman!

Thank you, Lance!

I shared Lance's communication with Jane. She was surprised at the cat's insistence about how much he loved her and how he was simply waiting for her to really understand how amazing she is. She acknowledged the truth of his words and vowed to work on opening herself to her lovability, and not to pin it on him with his shifting behavior. She really saw how he was shifting depending on how she was being with herself. For instance, if she was feeling a bit low about herself, he would pull away or be aloof. Then she would look at him and say to herself, "He doesn't love me, he just walked away!" Then everything he did or didn't do would "mean" something about her. She reflected on how when she was feeling good about herself, he was right with her and very attentive.

In the moment of Jane's reflective thought of her cat's closeness and how it correlated with her positive self-esteem, there was a shift in her expression. I asked her about it. She said, "Maia, he really does love me! I really get what he is saying—he's right! When I'm putting myself down, he stays away. And when he stays away, I acknowledge to myself that I am right, I am not worthy of his love, that he does not love me. I see now that he does love me and that I am loveable. It is my own point of view about myself that sometimes says otherwise. He loves me no matter what! I will no longer put that on him, and I am going to love myself and stop this nonsense! I can really change this! I am excited! Thank you, Maia! Thank you, Lance!"

The next time I visited their home a few months later, Jane and Lance were sitting close together on the couch, obviously enjoying one another's company tremendously

CHAPTER SIX

A Blue Miracle

I t was a blustery fall morning in northern Arizona. We'd had more than a week of cold, stormy weather, beginning with a tremendous hailstorm. Today the wind was blowing and there were snow flurries. I happened to be out at the barn finishing up my chores when I received an urgent call from a woman named Susan. She was very worried about her cat, who had somehow gotten outside during the hailstorm about eight days ago. Andy was a Blue Point Siamese who had never been outside before. Susan had only moved to Arizona about six months ago and now her cat was out in a remote area with few houses in severe weather with the possibility of encountering many coyotes, mountain lions, eagles, hawks and other predators. Susan was frantic, and I totally understood why this was so upsetting for her.

I decided to have at least a short conversation with her cat right then, so I took a few moments to find a place at the barn to get comfortable and then I began to reach out to Andy by saying hello to him in my head.

Hello, Andy.

The cat responded immediately.

Hello?!

Andy, are you OK?

He responded in a funny way, like he had to think about my question for a few moments. In the silence, I really got from him that he was taking in his experience and trying to come up with a way to describe it as well as how he was doing.

He said: *I guess?*

Then I thought to ask Andy the question I pose to missing animals so that I may determine for their people right away whether they are dead or alive, and that is, "Are you alive and well in your physical body—the one known to the person who has contacted me?" Animals can go on and on talking with us enthusiastically about many things and never mention the fact that they have died. They don't generally bring up death as a topic about themselves because they don't see themselves as ever dying in the way that we do. They tend to think of their physical body as being something like a costume. It is not who they are, and they know that they themselves never die—only the body dies. When they are dead from our perspective, they are not dead at all from theirs.

Whether we think of them as being dead or alive, animals are always accessible to talk with us, and even when they are dead, they will often share in a joyous and enthusiastic manner that can have us naturally assuming they are alive. Why would we even consider that they could be dead when they are so alive in their way of sharing—more alive than how most people who are alive share? But after talking with them a little longer, they may excitedly tell us in great detail about how they made their transition of death. That may happen if something about the transition of the body was a crucial part of the story they happened to be telling; otherwise, we may never hear of their death unless we ask them.

So I asked Andy the question:

Are you alive and well in your body, the one known to Your Woman?

To this he instantly responded:

YES!

Good! Are you injured?

No.

Andy felt amazingly stable to me, despite the craziness of his circumstances being out of doors for the first time and in one of our worst winter storms. He did not seem overly afraid nor was he desperate to get home. He was obviously finding some satisfaction in the experience of being out on his own.

I thought I would ask him some questions about where he was and what he was seeing. I happened to know the area where he'd gone missing and that there were only two other houses nearby. A few miles down the dirt road there was a loop road of houses and otherwise, the only other building nearby was an old homestead situated at the base of canyon cliff walls. That house had become a Forest Service ranger station for some Native

American rock art and cliff dwellings.

Picturing the area in my mind, I asked the cat what he saw from his vantage point.

Andy, are you near houses?

Yes.

From where you are, can you see more than one house?

Yes.

This meant he had to be either near his own home and the two neighbors, or near the loop road where there are a number of homes.

Do you know where your own home is?

I think so.

Do you want to come home?

Yes!

We were in a nice steady flow of questions and responses and then I asked him my next question: Andy, are you ready to come home right now?

To this I did not receive an instant response. It was as if he were pondering my question and trying to decide how he wanted to respond.

I wouldn't have imagined him having fun out there in this rugged weather, but I have learned that animals have an entirely different way of looking at things and it is not good for me to assume anything; really, it is best for me to come from a very open place, eager to hear whatever it is they wish to share. So I asked another question.

Andy, are you having any fun being out of doors?
To this he responded instantly and clearly:

Yes, I am having a grand adventure! But I do want to come home at some point.

I could feel the new sense of aliveness he felt in being out of doors. Despite the weather challenges, he was actually having a fulfilling experience and he wanted more.

I smiled, feeling his satisfaction. And then I thought about Susan and how upset and worried she was. I wanted to be sure Andy knew what Susan and her husband were going through.

Andy, your people are very worried about you and they want to find you and have you home.

I know!

He suddenly became very serious. He shifted from a playful adventurer to being concerned and thoughtful, and then he said:

It is important that my humans know that they did not do anything wrong. I was planning an adventure and looking for an opportunity to escape for a long time. I love them and I don't want them to be punishing themselves because I am away from home.

Do you want to be found right now?

With this question there was the silence from him again; he

was obviously thinking. And then he suddenly responded.

I want to come home, but I am not quite ready. I have some more adventuring to do.

Where are you right now?

I'm hiding out in some bushes. I am a little scared and just holding tight for the moment.

Andy, it sounds like you are near your house. Is that true?

Yes!

Will you tell me exactly where you are so your Woman can come out and get you?

There was that silence again! I was noticing it and then suddenly Andy said:

I just want her to know I am safe and that I love her. I'm doing exactly what I want to do and I am not ready to come in yet. I want her to relax and focus on other things in her life. I want them to not blame each other for leaving the door open. I want to have the freedom to have my experience.

Andy, is there anything else you want?

Some food would be great! She can put some out for me. Ask my Woman to be open to a miracle.

OK, let me talk with your Woman.

I called Susan back and began to tell her about my conversation with Andy.

Maia, go ahead, tell me what you found out.
She was bracing herself for the worst.

Susan, Andy assures me he is doing well.

Maia, how could he be doing well when he's been out in this weather for eight days?! If he's still alive he is obviously near death by now. I doubt he's even alive, but I must say, I love hearing that he's alive. I would like to hope that he is!

He assures me that he is alive, and that he actually had been looking for a way to escape and explore the great outdoors for quite some time now. He's actually enjoying this! And he does plan to come home eventually.

Maia, this is hard for me to believe! Looking at the weather and knowing he's never been outside before, let alone in this kind of a storm. I don't even want to go out!

I see what you are saying Susan, and this is what I am hearing from him. He actually feels good to me. Are you putting any food out for him?

No, I was afraid I might attract some other wild animals to the house.

I would suggest you put out food near the house, for instance, on a patio or near an entryway. You might consider leaving your garage door open as well in case he wants to come in.

OK.

It sounds like he is very near your house hiding in the bushes, but I would encourage you to put up flyers by the homes on the loop road to the south of you, and consider going door to door with the flyers and talking with your neighbors as well. There is the ranger station too. Be sure everyone knows you are looking for him. Also, you could put up flyers on the main dirt road. Right now he is in one place but he could become mobile at any time.

OK, I will do this. Are you sure he's alive?

Yes, I am quite sure! One last thing, Susan, Andy asks that you be open to a miracle.

Wow! Put that way, I can only say yes!

I believe he is actually very close to your home and I would suggest that you continue to look in the bushes and near your buildings, and talk with your nearest neighbors. Also, I would encourage you to notify the Humane Society if you haven't already.

We have talked with the staff at the Humane Society and we put an ad in the newspaper. I will talk with the neighbors and put out some flyers.

OK Susan, you are doing all you can. Remember to continue focusing on other things of life as well. Relax as much as possible and clear up any upset between you and your husband over the door being left open. Call me if you have other questions.

I will Maia, all right. Thanks.

I called Susan a few days later. It had now been nearly two weeks since her cat escaped from the house, and still no Andy.

A BLUE MIRACLE

Susan was in the process of accepting Andy's death and was not too interested in hearing that he was still alive. I reminded her of Andy's request that she believe in a miracle. I could hear a tiny thread of hope in her voice, but she was already looking to give another cat an opportunity to be adopted and come in to take Andy's position.

Meanwhile, Andy assured me he was doing just fine, but was still not ready to come home.

I felt compelled to ask him about his people and their lack of belief that he could be alive.

Don't worry! All is well. Their focus has shifted to their own lives, exactly as I requested. I now have the freedom to really experience my adventure without all their concerns and upset. I have a peaceful journey now!

What do you think about them looking for another cat to adopt?

I am not concerned, nor offended. I want them to go on living and a part of that is to go on loving—to love another, and to be loved. I totally understand this and I am fully in acceptance of what they are doing.

What if when you return there is another cat there in your place?

No problem! I will simply come back into their lives and we will have another cat as well. She really wants another cat anyway.

So what now, Andy?

Simply let her know what you are communicating with me and let that be it. All you can do is share what you hear from me. My needs are less now because the weather is warming.

OK, Andy, I will let her know.

A week later, I was at the barn brushing my horse Delight, when I heard the phone ring. I asked Delight to please excuse me and I answered the phone.

It was Susan, who excitedly shared the news that Andy had miraculously returned! She had been preparing to leave the house to go out of town when she heard her other cat crying in the direction of the porch. When she went to check on her, she noticed that her cat was looking out the window at something. It was Andy! He was there meowing and asking to come in. He was thin and had some cactus spines in his back, but otherwise, he was alive and well. He had lived out of doors during the worst storm of the winter, probably the worst storm we'd had in years.

Susan acknowledged that she had indeed experienced a miracle. She thanked me and then quickly got off the phone so she could take Andy to the veterinarian to check him out.

Losing our pets can be the most difficult thing a human being ever faces. And some true miracles can occur when we find that our animals are more resourceful than we might imagine. Knowing Andy and what he accomplished in his quest for adventure was truly admirable, and yet it pushed his humans to some profound limits too.

I was curious to ask Andy more about his adventure, but even before I could form my first question, Andy began to share his experience with me.

I explored and I explored! I took in the smells and the sensations. I loved the smell of the Earth and loved to roll in it. I loved climbing small trees! I always intended to go home, so it wasn't that big a deal to me.

Andy, do you realize you could have been eaten by a coyote or some other wild animal?

Yes I do, and at the same time it was totally worth it. The experience I had has enriched my life beyond what I can really explain. But I will give it a try! I feel so confident in myself. I feel so grounded and stable now too! I was always thinking of leaving to do this adventure, but never took action. Now that I have taken the action, I feel fulfilled and no longer feel the need to take this action again. I am eager to settle back in and enjoy my daily adventures right here!

Thank you, Andy!

Thank you, Woman! I appreciate you talking with my people. It helped keep them at ease and sent them on a path, which gave me the opportunity to be really free out there so I could come home. I look thin, but I feel GREAT!!!

Excellent! I am happy for you Andy!

CHAPTER SEVEN

The World's Best Mom

Since 1997, with the wonders of ever advancing technology, I have had the great pleasure to communicate with people from around the world. I have experienced the joy of being in so many amazing places and, at the same time, offering my People, Pet and Nature Communication consultations and classes.

I have many fond memories of sitting in a comfy chair in the entrance of my tent looking out on glorious mountains, rivers and valleys, and using my phone and a recording device to talk with clients as far away as Gibraltar and Japan.

With my adventurous lifestyle and my love of the outdoors, this work has been fantastic because I can take it wherever I go. The only place where I was really limited in doing my work was when I lived in Ecuador for nearly three years, specifically in the Galapagos Islands and the Amazon Jungle. That was clearly, for me, a situation of getting some help from Spirit in remembering the importance of focusing my attention right there where I was.

The way Spirit worked for me was that on numerous occasions, I remember eagerly walking the sandy streets in the tiny village of Puerto Vilamil on the island of Isabella, to the telephone company, to call home in the States. Halfway there, time after time, I would meet an Italian man I was trying to avoid. He was on his way back from the phone company and he would always tell me that, for no reason he could understand, the telephone company was shut down that day. This was really bad news for me because I was missing my family and friends and realizing that there was no way I could continue with my work with clients around the world.

Whenever we met, he would speak to me in Italian, of which I understood very little, but I soon realized that he wanted me to marry him. He relentlessly pursued me and to sweeten the deal, he promised that we could live together in the Galapagos forever. Our meetings along the sandy streets of the village were a source of both frustration and humor for me.

The phone systems were unreliable in the Galapagos and so was the Internet! There were only a few miraculous moments when I was actually able to get online and just as suddenly, I was offline for no reason anyone understood.

The islands themselves were rather elusive as well, and sometimes they were shrouded in dense clouds, making them seemingly non-existent. There are numerous historical reports of ships traveling through the Galapagos and never even seeing them because at the time they passed the islands, they were mysteriously hidden. That was how connecting with the outside world was for me while I was there.

In hindsight, accepting the way it was and having gratitude for connecting miraculously when I did was a true gift. As challenging as it was initially to set aside how I thought it should be and what I knew and what I thought I knew, simply being there and experiencing the magic of all the species was truly amazing for me! All my memories of the people, animals and Nature in their island glory will never be forgotten.

The Amazon was another place where I gave up any hope of having contact with other regions of the world, let alone the nearest village on the edge of the jungle.

During my time in Ecuador, I eventually surrendered and focused on my own personal development, and my communication with the amazing animals, plants, sea creatures, the Earth and the precious human beings there.

Today, with the scope of what's possible technologically and because I live in a place with pretty good access, I find myself meeting wonderful people from around the world. For example, in recent weeks I have communicated with people from Thailand, The Dominican Republic, Korea and Canada. Last week I was sitting at my desk in Sedona, Arizona on a Skype call with a couple from Cape Town, South Africa. I fell in love with them right away and it was so great to share those moments together. Meanwhile, during our call, I was talking with their dogs telepathically and sharing with the couple what their dogs had to say. Toward the end of our conversation, they brought the dogs over one at a time to their computer screen so I could see them. It was so much fun!

The really interesting thing about doing telepathic communication with animals and our neighbors in Nature is that the actual communication requires no technology whatsoever! It happens with the miraculous capacity of a living being's body, mind and spirit. When I think of all the sophisticated technological tools I use today to stay in contact, and the simplicity of telepathic com-

117

munication, it truly is amazing! And it always works! I love the simplicity of it as well as the power that this kind of communication has to transform situations that may otherwise go on causing pain and confusion for a lifetime.

Ninety-nine percent of the time I am working telepathically with people and their animals from out of state, or out of the country where we don't have the opportunity to meet in person. Despite the physical distance that separates us, the interactions with my clients are so precious and memorable that our meetings often forever change our lives.

I enjoy meeting with clients in person too, and experience that on a fairly regular basis when some of my clients plan to meet me while they visit Sedona.

Last week, I traveled about 35 miles to the nearby town of Flagstaff because it was important to my client that I meet with her pets in person. When I arrived at her home, Jennifer introduced me to two of her pets. Her cat Lily was resting in her little bed on the living room floor. Her other cat Savannah was in the back bedroom and Jennifer said she would bring her out for me to talk with later. Ginger, her dog, was at the neighbor's house and she explained that she would go get her once we had talked with the cats.

Jennifer also shared with me that she had never done anything like this before, and that she was a little nervous. Interestingly, I detected a sense of vulnerability all around, including within myself. It seemed like each of us—myself, Jennifer and her two cats and dog—were open to what might transpire that would make a difference.

I shared with Jennifer a little bit about how telepathic communication works and then she went to get Savannah. As Jennifer walked back into the living room with her rather large grey tabby cat in her arms, I could see that Savannah was obviously very uncomfortable and doing everything she could to pull away. Even after Jennifer was sitting in her recliner, the cat wouldn't settle down on her lap. Actually, Jennifer was trying with all her might to hold onto the reluctant cat.

Jennifer told me that ever since she brought Ginger into the family fours years ago, Savannah refused to be in the living room or any area of the house where the dog was. Jennifer was heartbroken over Savannah wanting to retreat to the bedroom all the time, and she said she felt she'd hurt Savannah and their relationship by bringing Lily and Ginger into the family. At the same time, Jennifer loved them and could not imagine not having them there too.

In talking with Savannah, I actually had the unexpected experience of the cat being very much at peace. She was not in any way angry or disappointed with Jennifer; in fact, she loved her dearly and really wanted Jennifer to know this. In reality, she actually loved Lily too, and even Ginger. The thing was this: Jennifer's belief that she did Savannah wrong was an invitation for the cat to act out that belief as being true, and as long as Jennifer continued to believe that she had failed the cat and let her down, Savannah said she would go on acting as if it were true.

As I sat there on the couch, my attention was repeatedly drawn to a collage of pictures across the way of an adorable boy, and I kept thinking to ask about him.

Finally, Jennifer let Savannah get away and she immediately ran back into the other room. With a small sigh, she said, "Let's talk with Lily now."

After I talked with Lily, the interesting thing that stood out

for me from both cats was that they both thought Jennifer was
the most amazing woman in the world! They absolutely adored
her and in return, she was devoted to their care. They were es-
sentially her children, and she was so precious to them. Lily had
some dietary requests which Savannah asked for as well, and then
Jennifer went off to her neighbor's to get Ginger, who turned out
to be a little dynamo! She was a tiny Schnauzer mix who literally
jumped up and down in the air a number of times just for fun
before she would launch herself missle-like onto the couch. The
jumps were like test flights before the final launch! No wonder
the cats were a little bug-eyed with the energy and dynamics of
this little dog. But at the same time, I was reminded by the cats
that they actually liked Ginger. And Savannah even went on to
say that bringing Lily and Ginger into their home was the best
thing Jennifer had ever done—it brought life and fun and excitement and responsibility.

During my conversations, I kept noticing the photos of the
boy, but felt hesitant to initiate a conversation about him. Then,
in the midst of my thoughts I suddenly heard Jennifer say, "My
son passed away about ten years ago." I knew this was the boy
I was seeing. Her eyes welled up like it had happened yesterday
and now I noticed that he was talking. With telepathic communication, you can talk with anyone and he had simply joined our
conversation.

In listening to him share, I was brought powerfully to the
awareness of how precious life is and how important it is for
us to be thoughtful and to stay balanced and focused, and how
challenging that can be for any one of us at times. He had made
a momentary choice that resulted in his death. I was struck by the
tragedy of how this precious young man and his amazing Mom

had been separated so suddenly. He was an intelligent, responsible and attractive young man with a huge heart, and Jennifer's favorite person in the world.

He said that he wanted his Mom to stop blaming herself and to know that he now understood everything she ever told him. He went on to say that he loved her dearly and was right there with her in Spirit. Nothing would make him happier than seeing her fulfilled and happy. He knew that she believed she'd let him down like she thought she was letting her cats and dog down and that she thought she was not a good mother because otherwise, he would be there now, safe with her.

After receiving this information, I had an even greater understanding of Savannah's behavior. By hiding out in the bedroom day after day, she was pressing Jennifer to do something about it. But it wasn't about Savannah, it was about Jennifer blaming herself for her son's death. Savannah was actually helping Jennifer believe that she was a "bad" Mom so that Jennifer would get help in order to realize that her son loved her dearly and that he made a choice that had resulted in his death, a choice he now regretted but accepted.

It wasn't her fault. She wasn't a bad Mom! Unfortunately there was nothing that could bring her son back, but her cats and dog and son all wanted her to know the truth of their love and appreciation for her. I shared this with Jennifer and she looked at me with tears in her eyes. I was teary too!

As I was heading out the door to go home, I thought to show Jennifer photos of my 4-legged family—my horse Delight and goat, Chanella. And then Jennifer invited me back inside. She showed me all around her home. We went from room to room where there were pictures of her precious son from the time he was a little boy until he was a teenager and young adult.

I felt so honored to get to know him through her sharing and the way she opened up with me. I naturally liked her son and as she talked, he was very present with us too.

After I had seen all the photos, we were standing in the living room saying our goodbyes when we suddenly noticed to our amazement that Savannah was on the couch lying on her back with her front and back legs comfortably stretched out in opposite directions like she hadn't stretched in years. She was obviously at ease with no fear whatsoever! It was wonderful to see her relaxing like this with such obvious satisfaction. Meanwhile, Ginger was nearby resting and Lily was there too!

Jennifer spoke out in amazement and explained that Savannah had not been in the same room with Ginger since the dog came into their family four years ago. This was an entirely remarkable event to see the cat there, so comfortable and so relaxed!

On my way home, I felt a tremendous sense of gratitude at having been a part of something as profound as what I had just experienced and thinking of the preciousness of this woman and her amazing pets and son who all absolutely adored her.

A little later in the day, I called Jennifer to check on her. She shared that after I left, she had the most beautiful afternoon where all three of her beloved pets peacefully lounged in the living room together for two and a half hours and only moved when a mail delivery person came to the door. She then shared how she was beginning to understand that, to them, she is and will always be the World's Best Mom!

CHAPTER EIGHT

A Whole New World

I t was a sunny Tuesday morning and I had just returned from my walk in the Red Rocks and was settling in at my desk to take a look at my list of appointments for the day. My first call was to be with a woman named Nora who had set up our telephone meeting through my website with my online appointment scheduler.

Nora and I had never met, nor had we talked on the phone before; in her appointment notes she wrote that she'd found me while reading *Spirituality and Health Magazine* that had featured an article about my work and she said that what she read really resonated with her. She also loved the photo of me in the magazine with Red the horse who was being silly, opening his mouth as he was talking to me. Nora said she knew she wanted to talk with me, so she set up an appointment right away.

The main purpose in setting up our meeting was to have me talk with her cat about bronchitis-type symptoms, which had been going on for a number of months. In addition, Nora wanted me to look in on why she herself had been experiencing heart palpitations for about four weeks now.

As is my routine, before calling Nora I took a few minutes to get to know her cat, Bunny. Then, just as it turned 9:00 AM, as scheduled, I dialed Nora's telephone number.

Hello Nora, it's Maia Kincaid calling for our appointment. Do you have any questions for me before we begin?

Hello Maia! I really don't know what to say and I have no idea how you do your work.

Well Nora, let me give you some information on the overall process and then you can let me know if you have any questions. Does that sound good?

Yes! Thank you, Maia!

Nora, I talk with the animals telepathically—I can say hello to them from afar without ever having met them before. I have a conversation with the animal similar to how it is when I call a person on the phone with whom I have not met before. It is important that I share with you that this is something humans have the natural ability to do. I am not unlike other humans, only I spend a lot of time communicating in this way.

I have already been talking with Bunny telepathically for a few minutes before making my call to you. I could go ahead and share with you my conversation with Bunny from my notes so far, and then you will have an idea of what's possible with telepathic communication, and from there I can respond to any additional questions you might like to ask. Does that sound good?

Yes, Maia, please go ahead! I am eager to hear what Bunny had to say!

First, Nora let me ask you, are you seeing a doctor, and is Bunny under the care of a veterinarian?

Yes, Maia and they gave us some medicines and some suggestions that seemed to help at first, but then we were back where we started.

Thank you, Nora. I do suggest continuing to work with the doctors to monitor both your and Bunny's health.

Will do!

OK Nora, just before I called you I sat quietly and said hello to Bunny in my head and she immediately said hello back to me. Then I decided to ask her some questions so I could get to know her. Here's how our dialog went.

Bunny, tell me about yourself.

I am a wise and loving goddess!

I got that!

I could feel Bunny's confidence, grace, and even her sense of ease in being.
I asked: How are you feeling?

I feel a little heaviness in my chest and some scratchiness when I breathe, but it is not really that bad.

Is there anything your Woman can do to help you feel better?

YES!!!

Great, feel free to share what that is Bunny, and I will pass the information along to her.

We are stuck!

What do you mean?

Just that, we are stuck! She feels trapped, and so do I!

What has you and your woman feeling trapped?

Well, we cannot leave where we are and we cannot be free.

Do you want to leave?

YES!!! And so does she!

How long has this been going on?

Years!

Why haven't you moved?

I cannot get my woman to take steps in that direction. She thinks about it often and dreams about it, but when it comes to taking ANY real action, she actually settles back in deeper and seems to get even more stuck!

Is she trying to run from something?

Yes, herself. She is up against one of the biggest obstacles for people—she is resisting getting really close to another human being. She is also resisting being vulnerable and intimate with herself, with this man and maybe with others as well.

Bunny, please share more.

First, let me say that she is not the only one. I too, am in resistance and so is our other human here. I am resisting going deeper with each of them as well. Basically, none of us are living freely, fully expressed and with our hearts open, the way we would love to live.

We are all guarded! He is guarded because he doesn't want to get hurt—again. On the surface, she is avoiding loving him. Underneath it all, the big fear is of loving and honoring herself.

She has a new freedom that she does not even realize, but instead of doing what she always dreamed with this new freedom, she is keeping herself busy thinking of how to escape what seems like an impossible situation. It is like she is at a precipice ready to leap into a new life and a new reality, and her muscles are taut and tired from staying in this position ready to take action for so long, but no action is ever really taken. This no-win position is what is causing her anxiety and heart palpitations. She makes it very uncomfortable to live. Her very existence at home is either a reaction or response to something he is or is not doing. She places him under a microscope and filters her world through a lens with an attitude of, "Now what?!" She views him with a focus on the reasons of why not to get close. Hence she doesn't get close, and then feels the need to justify her lack of desire for closeness and to defend against it.

She has all sorts of ideas about who he is and what he wants. And she has reactions to this story she created about him. Meanwhile, he is not the person she thinks he is. He is not pressuring her to be something or someone she is not. He really likes her true self and he really loves sharing his life with her. This whole focus drives her crazy and is not at all what she really wants to think about, but it is what she thinks about to avoid fulfilling her dreams.

I responded: OK, I think I understand most of what you are saying, but I have some questions. Are you open to answering some questions, Bunny?

Of course! Go ahead!

OK, what is this new freedom Nora has?

Good question! She actually is in a situation where she is living with this man who she loves more than she realizes.

Because it is her home they share, she feels somewhat invaded, but the reality is that she has a good companion who could be a great companion—even an ideal companion—if she would allow herself to really know him, instead of the story she created about who she thinks he is. She also has a unique living situation that could allow her to do all the things she has long dreamed of that she currently can't do because she's working and too busy and then too tired or uninspired. Her unfulfilled dreams await her! But instead of honoring and rewarding herself for creating this opportunity, she actually has spent the entire time and all of her energy creating wedges between herself and this man. Her dream is literally before her, right under her nose, and yet she is scrambling to get out and get away from a wondrous creation that she worked so hard to bring to reality. She feels trapped in her own home, in her own creation! And, being so close to her, I feel trapped too! I have heaviness and sadness in my lungs even though I myself am not really sad, and in reality am at peace. I know I am not trapped; I simply feel that way because I so identify with her.

It is important to me that it is perfectly clear to my Woman that she did not cause my illness—she did not create or cause it! I am simply expressing and demonstrating what I am experiencing from her. I am giving an expression of it for my Woman to see and intimately experience. It is for the possibility of doing good for her that I take this on.

We animals often do this for our people because of our love and appreciation for them, and to help facilitate learning and development of the heart and spirit of the human.

My Woman has an enormous heart, but she is withholding love both from herself and from this man here in the house. If she opens herself to loving him and his love for her, she opens herself to love itself—to loving herself.

Bunny, what is it your Woman dreams to do?

Her main interests are to create art, explore her natural healing abilities, and she would love to share her life with the man of her dreams.

She has the time and place to do this now, Bunny?

Yes, if she would accept love and his gift she would have the time for sure, and the place is so easy to set up—it is right there! Let me give you an example to help you understand. It is as if she received an inheritance that changed her financial status so that she could live freely without needing to work outside the home, and say this happened a year and a half ago. But, instead of stopping to reassess her life and change direction accordingly, she has continued on working and living as she has for years. She's in denial of her new possibilities, and instead of fulfilling her long held dreams; she's spending her time and energy in negativity thinking of reasons to keep her distance from this man she loves.

If she were to allow herself to focus on the exploration of her creativity and natural healing abilities, she would be overflowing with joy and gratitude and the creativity of creation itself. She may even want to experience and celebrate intimacy with her man, but it is not necessary. All that is necessary is for her to accept her gift. It is there, awaiting her.

Bunny, what is this gift?

The gift is the opportunity for her to have the time, energy and freedom to create art and healing. Her man would like her to have this opportunity, but he does not know how to tell her and have her get it.

Bunny, let me confirm something. So basically, Nora is in a position where she is living with a man she loves but does not want to get too close, either emotionally or physically.

Yes!

And, that she has longed to quit her work and allow him to support her in this way. And he is asking nothing in return for this opportunity, other than to live there with her and to be her companion in life.

Bunny, it sounds like you believe they have a good relationship and that he is someone who really cares about her and for her. She really does care about him and for him, and she provides a home for him, but she thinks she has to do everything on her own and not accept his help.

So, what you are saying is that Nora's dream is right there and she simply does not see it.

Yes! And that this is a common thing with you humans.

What do you mean?

We animals see this with you humans all the time! You want something so badly and then it is there in front of you for years and years, as you continue to struggle and dream like it is nowhere to be seen! We wonder why you don't simply take the opportunities that come along as a response to your prayers. Your prayers are so often acknowledged and fulfilled instantly, but it is like your eyes are closed or something!

Wow! I have a very weird sense that this is probably true, and now I am having an image of a hamster running at top speed on a wheel wanting to get to a particular place and passing it by repeatedly while running around in circles. Ouch! The reality of this hurts!

Yikes! Now I feel like I need a little time to simply be with this reality. Actually, what I really want is to forget about it for a while until I am ready to embrace the truth. But this particular conversation is not supposed to be about me!

I paused for a moment to regroup. OK, Bunny I'm back. What do you suggest for your Woman?

I suggest that she stop resisting and fighting! She can stop by simply slowing down and being more conscious of herself throughout her day. For instance, it is important that she take note of how she is thinking, feeling and being. That she turn her focus toward herself and on being conscious and aware, as opposed to keeping her focus on me and our man.

When she notices she's feeling uncomfortable she can ask

herself, "What is this all about?" She will immediately have some ideas about why she is feeling this way, and then she can simply choose to be aware of her changing moods and feelings. She will notice by noticing that the moods and ways of being pass and change quickly.

By paying attention, my Woman will even see how she may choose to create a particular mood. And she will see how she is already doing this and how she often chooses a mood that she doesn't even like. The mood is chosen by the point of view she has at the moment.

She has a negative point of view about this man, so the reality of what she experiences with him matches up with her belief of who he is, how he thinks, etc.

Meanwhile, she is living with an entirely different cat than she thinks she's living with! He is actually a rather cool cat! She would know it if she either had a good point of view about him or, better yet, if she had no point of view whatsoever and simply allowed him to show up as he does, so she appreciates him newly each time.

OK, well um, Bunny, I have a number of questions. In a simple, step-by-step process, how do you recommend that she change the way she has been with her negative point of view about him, and how can she make it a positive or neutral point of view?

First, it is important that she recognizes her point of view, simply by turning her attention onto herself and becoming aware of it. It is also important that she not punish or think poorly of herself when she notices the negativity.

It is also important that she remembers she is not her point of view. Her viewpoint is not necessarily who she is or the way *she really wants to be. It is simply a habit, and with this habit she has created what seems like an impossible and unpleasant situation that she cannot break free from.*

In reality, she has created a story about her circumstances that is not really true.

If she is willing to look at it as simply a creation—a story— she will have a whole new experience of her day-to-day life. And with that will come a new sense of freedom and ease that can have her relax, settle in and really assess her life from a powerful and peaceful state of mind. Then she can make any changes she likes. She will realize that she has access to new materials and that she can clear her canvas and create anew. Her story is actually a creation of her imagination, which desperately seeks expression through writing and artistic creation. It is getting some expression through a biased view of her daily life.

Does this make sense to you, Woman?

Yes. So basically, if she is willing to look at her life from the standpoint of the possibility that all that she believes is not necessarily true, and if she is willing to set aside her point of view or her story on things, if only for a few minutes to see what else may be revealed or understood, then she will have access to awareness that perhaps what she has dreamed of is right before her eyes, and what she thinks is true may not be true at all.

If she is willing to consider other possibilities, a blank canvas for instance, or even simply allowing herself to be quiet for a moment, she might experience another truth or the real truth. Reminds me of the movie *The Matrix*!

You got it! From our perspective, humans tend to like to stick with what they think they know, even if they don't like it!

So many human associations and assumptions are made to have you feeling stable and secure but in reality, much of what you think and believe simply isn't true. If it made you happy we would suggest you keep it because we are committed to your happiness, but from our observation, it doesn't make you happy at all! I guess to be more precise I could say that it makes you THINK you are happy briefly, but it is not a true happiness. It is more like relief because it is something you think you know.

Our suggestion is that you loosen your hold on your beliefs and don't worry, because you will come back to believing without a problem. But by loosening them and being open to be informed otherwise, you open yourself to new possibilities, new awareness, new life and feeling alive. It could be that you experience this as you return to a belief, knowing it stronger than ever. It could be that you feel this knowing you are loved and that you deserve to be loved and that you will have whatever you desire in life.

Bottom line, take off your lenses as best you can on a daily or even a minute-by-minute basis. Look at your world with the newest eyes you can muster, with any old beliefs acknowledged and set aside, if even for a few moments. This is how a new world is created and how life is celebrated minute-by-minute, day after day!

I like this Bunny! OK, I will share this with your Woman.

So, Nora, that's how my conversation went with Bunny!

Wow, Maia! I am amazed at how she shared with you! I feel

like a bridge between my confusion and being free has suddenly appeared. What you have shared and what she has shared really

makes sense! I do love this man, but I find myself judging him
and practically looking for things to berate him about. It's like
there is this force within me that wants to attack him and keep
him at a distance. In reality, I really do love him and I would
love to have him close. I am continually pushing him away and
thinking he cannot be my dream man because of this or that. I
have difficulty really finding any good reason to not be close, but I
continue to avoid being close with him.

I feel so relieved—it is exhausting being like this! I just want to
hug him and say I'm sorry!

No wonder my heart is palpitating!

This is so great, Nora! I sense that you are feeling free and
alive and joyful once again!

Yes!

I suddenly heard the cat interrupting my exchange with Nora.
Excuse me, Nora. Bunny has something she wants to say. I
took a moment to listen to Bunny.

Nora, remember when Bunny mentioned that you were in a
place in your life where you had new freedom and that you could
at last focus on and fulfill some of the aspirations you have been
dreaming of for a long time?

Yes, I remember this Maia!

Bunny wanted me to remind you that you are in a position-
where you can at last stop working and focus on fulfilling your
dreams, but now that you have this new freedom, you are feeling
more stuck and less free than ever.

This is true!

Bunny says that many of us humans have dreams we desperately wish to fulfill, yet we continue to struggle, waiting for the opportune time or place to fulfill them. In fact, Bunny actually said that humans frequently continue to struggle while an opportunity is right there awaiting them. And sometimes—OK, I am being corrected by Bunny. Not sometimes, it is actually often that we humans fail to realize our opportunities, and we continue to struggle and dream, and struggle and dream, year after year after year!

Bunny says that you are in a position like that right now. She says you are so busy feeling stuck and believing you are stuck that you fail to see the opportunity you have to really feel peaceful and joyful in your home, in your relationship and in your life.

Before I could say another word, Nora quickly spoke.

Oh, that is so true! I really am negative and sometimes it feels really good to be negative!

Bunny is asking me to tell you that when you are negative, it is not necessarily who you are; it is simply the way you are choosing to be in the moment. Being this way does not necessarily lead to wonderful feelings, but it is actually a choice. She invites you to try on a new point of view. Allow yourself to have some fun, and to laugh and enjoy your life.

Nora laughed and then said: It all makes sense! Thank you, Maia! And thank you, Bunny!

Thank you, Nora! And Bunny, thank you so much! I have a new awareness and a new perspective on my own world after hearing what you had to say. Thank you! Thank you!

And then Bunny said:

A WHOLE NEW WORLD

You are both very welcome!

The next morning as I was beginning my day, I began to think of Bunny and feel the presence of her there with me. I said hello to her and asked why she was with me.

I want you to call my Woman.

OK, tell me what you would like me to talk with her about.

I want her to know that I love her dearly and I am very proud of her.

I called Nora and shared Bunny's message of love for her and how proud she was of her human.

Nora excitedly shared: Maia, you know after we talked yesterday, I felt so much better! I had a new sense of ease and we actually had a very nice evening. I see what Bunny is saying and I am going to really go with this. I really get it!
Thank you so much for your call and for talking with Bunny! I feel a whole new sense of freedom and fun in my life already. I am eager to experience love now! Thank Bunny for me. I don't know what else to say. This has been amazing!

Thank you, Nora! I too, am touched by what we have experienced. And, I feel so grateful too! Thank you and thank you, Bunny!

CHAPTER NINE

Cats and Coons

When we began to talk, I remembered Ani Serena's dedication to animals and her passion for animals having their voice. She was a Buddhist nun and certainly lived up to the teachings of compassion that is common to her faith. Previously, we had talked with her dog and came up with some solutions for several odd challenges he was having adjusting to life in her home after years of fending for himself on the street. This time Ani Serena called to request that I talk with the feral cats and raccoons who congregated near the temple.

The members of the Buddhist temple had designed and built a small attractive house on the property that served as shelter where feral cats could come in out of the weather and find food, water and a bed. The cats were thrilled with the arrangement. Whenever possible, the nuns would capture cats and take them to their veterinarian to be spayed and neutered and cared for in whatever way needed. This was but one of the numerous programs the members participated in that benefitted animals. Everything went beautifully in the new cat house until recently when a Momma raccoon showed up with some of her young. Once the coons discovered the cat house, they returned on a regular basis and brought friends and family members.

Ani Serena explained the dilemma of the members. They wanted to provide for all the cats and for the raccoons too, but the cats were being pushed out of their house by the raccoons. Finding a way to be a compassionate listener for all of them and keep their original guests safe and happy was the subject of our call today.

Ani Serena had a list of the feral cats we would talk with as well as the raccoons to see if there was some sort of a solution to the dilemma.

Just before calling Ani Serena, I took a few moments to say hello to the cats and the raccoons.

I said hello silently in my head to the cats as a group. I was greeted by lively, vivacious and youthful hellos, even though some of the cats were up in years. They were clearly happy to be featured in this conversation and they loved their cat house with all its comfortable arrangements. They let me know they were interested in coming up with a solution that would have their home available in the future. They actually had a plan they thought would work and they were eager to share it.

Because I only had about thirty seconds before my telephone call with Ani Serena, I quickly said hello to the raccoons and had a similar response as I had from the cats. They were jovial and fun loving and they let me know they were honored to be having the opportunity to share their wishes and opinions.

By the time I was ready to call Ani Serena, I had a huge smile on my face. All of the cats and all of the raccoons were clearly eager for this upcoming meeting and the thing that I will never forget is that they were all so grateful both for the opportunity to meet and for what was already being provided by the members of the temple.

Once I was on the phone with Ani Serena, I shared how my conversations were going so far and she said:

Maia, this is so great! I am really eager to hear what they all say and see what we can do. We haven't come up with any workable ideas so far, so I am eager to hear what the animals have to say.

Excellent Ani Serena, let's talk with each of the cats individually to be sure that each one of them is on board with a plan that includes the raccoons, and then we can talk with the raccoons for the same purpose. How does that sound?

Great idea Maia!

Do you want to name the cats for me?

Sure, the first one has two names: Boy or Sammy.

OK, depending on who's talking with him, right?!

Yes!

OK Serena, let me be with this kitty for a moment. I am getting a lot of love from Boy for all of you, and for the arrangement. He loves having the freedom to be where he wants to be and also the food. He is open to have the coons around in the general area, but not right with him.

Maia, would he sleep in the cat house at night even if a rac-

141

coon comes in?

He's indicating that he would have a tendency to want to leave. He has respect for the raccoons and does not want to be there when they come in.

I have an idea of a plan that I got from the cats when I talked with them as a group just before I called you Serena, but let's check with the rest of them independently to be sure they are all in agreement.

OK.

Who's next?

King.

OK, King is actually getting something out of having the raccoons nearby. He actually thinks it is rather fascinating to have the raccoons living there. He is quite interested in these animals. King loves being at the temple grounds and he is there most of the time. There is no other place he wants to be!

That is true. King is always hanging around! Princess is next.

OK, Princess says she loves you, and that goes out to all of you there. And she definitely thinks of herself as a princess. She basically thinks of herself as being on a throne and that everyone else is there to serve her. She actually has the raccoons in that position as well. They could easily overtake her, but her demeanor has them stand back and give her space. Princess says that she does not mind them there as long as they continue to respect her boundaries. She says she is willing to work something out.

OK, who's next?

Little Man.

Little Man . . . this one is pure love.

Yes he is!

That's the first thing that comes to mind with him. He's often in a meditative state. Peacefulness, being grounded and radiating love are his interests. He really wants to work things out with the raccoons and thinks this is great example for us human beings, too.

He has not been neutered, Maia—is that alright? I'm sure he probably says yes.

He prefers it that way and at the same time he's actually open to being neutered if you can catch him! Catching him may be a challenge because he says you will have to be clever. He's not going to cooperate—you're on your own!

You've got that right! We've tried numerous times and so far he has eluded capture.

For not having been neutered, he is really amicable with other cats!

That is true, he is actually kind to the other cats—he doesn't get into fights.

He's in his own world. He's in a peaceful, meditative state.

Who is next, Ani Serena?

That would be Tony!

As she said his name, I heard Tony begin speaking to me. I relayed my experience to Ani Serena:

It's kind of funny. Tony likes to think of himself as being aggressive and tough. He likes to imagine getting into a tussle with the raccoons. It's sort of like a comic hero kind of fantasy for him because the reality is that he talks big but when the raccoons come close, he is the first cat to retreat. He does not realize the truth of where he stands. When I asked him if he would be willing to work something out with the raccoons, he sheepishly said he was.

Ani Serena burst out laughing and said:

That's Tony! Tony, we love you, sweet boy!

And then she said: OK, the next one is Momma Kitty. She's the Momma of some of the other cats.

Momma Kitty. She is like a rock, really solid. For her, having the coons around is no big deal. It's a normal daily occurrence. She does not mind sharing the space with the raccoons, and all seems to be well in the world for Momma Kitty! For her, these kinds of arrangements are what life's about. She is definitely open to have everything work for everyone.

Oh good! The next one, Maia, is Blossom.

Blossom is saying she loves all of you. She is well named! She reminds me of a blossom—very sweet.

Blossom acknowledges that she has some fear and concern about being close to the raccoons. She doesn't want to get real close. She's OK with working something out with them though. If the rest of the cats feel confident in a plan, she will go with it.

CATS AND COONS

I paused for a moment and Ani Serena said: OK, next is Dino. Now Maia, Dino comes and goes from the grounds—can you locate him to talk with him?

No problem. He is always connected to all of the humans involved there, even when he is out of sight for periods of time. As a matter of fact, he is already talking and sharing that the grounds are his primary home even though he is away for weeks at a time. He has numerous secondary locations that he frequents too. He is quite a charmer and has admirers wherever he goes! He says he works on the road and takes his work seriously. He's happy to have an arrangement for the cats and the coons!

That all sounds like Dino! I think he must have a girlfriend. He is another one that has not been neutered. He takes a week away then comes back.

It is true. He does have some girlfriends, some human admirers and lots of good places to be. He's quite the guy!

Yes he is!

The last one Maia, is Goldie. That's my cat. She's out with the feral cats during the day and comes in with me at night.

Ani Serena, she loves that arrangement! Its like she is being with her wild roots and then at the same time, has the joy of snuggling up with you. It's a fascinating adventure for her to live in two worlds, and quite rare for a cat. Goldie doesn't usually see the raccoons because they generally come to visit at night. She is open to whatever works well for her feral cat colleagues there.

OK, that pretty much covers the cats. Let me be with the coons for just a minute. There's one that comes by on a daily basis and others that make periodic visits.

That's true—there's the one I call Hazel, and then some others.

Let me be with them for a moment.

Sure.

You know, it is interesting. Sometimes when I talk with coons, they can be kind of bossy and their interest may be to simply go into an area and take the food and not be too concerned with working things out with other animals because they can simply go in and dominate, and everyone scatters.

But these coons are quite interested in having a relationship with the cats, and they actually say that they communicate with them. They also say they have a relationship with you humans, too. They are attracted to the energy there, and they really like the food as well.

I know they do! They eat a lot of food!

Yes! They actually are quite pleased with the whole picture.

Ani Serena, let's talk with the raccoons about what they are willing to work out, because I know it is super important to you that the cats not be run off from their home and that in particular, they have shelter in the winter months.

Yes, I want to be sure the cats have a place to be warm at night during the winter.

The raccoons say they understand, and now I have them and the cats together sharing ideas to have the Temple grounds be a sanctuary for all of them.

CATS AND COONS

OK, one thing that is coming to mind is to have another place to feed the cats.

Well, I haven't been putting the food in the cat house so much lately. I'm putting it on the porch instead. I did notice that someone went in the cat house recently and overturned everything. It was definitely a raccoon because it was done by an animal that has the use of their paws to grab things like the cat beds and actually flip them.

Yes! I do get that it was the coons that were in the cat house—that was their handiwork.

One of the suggestions from the cats and coons is to have the cat house be used strictly for sleeping and not have any food in there. The main conflict between the animals seems to be when they come together in this small space. The cats are there to sleep and eat, and the coons are there only to eat. But in those tight quarters, they get into conflict. The cats particularly feel threatened, and sometimes they are trapped and cannot get out past the raccoons once they have come in to eat.

The combined suggestion of the animals is that all of the food be kept and distributed a significant distance from the cat house, and that the cat house have a deep cleaning in order to clear away all food smells.

The animals may stay away for a brief period due to the disruption of their routine, but they will return.

The coons say they most likely will not go into the cat house as long as there are no food smells. And the coons don't need the cat house beds to sleep in—they have some cushy places to sleep. When they come around, they are simply looking for food and relationships.

The cats on the other hand, love the house and want the beds to sleep in. They really appreciate them and it makes a positive difference for them.

Wow, this is great Maia!

I agree! Looks like some new possibilities are opening up! Ani Serena, do you have a place a good distance away from the cat house where you could put the food?

I'll make one! I will clean out the cat house too! I'm so glad the coons know our concerns and it sounds like the cats and coons are all willing to work together. Normally they would just bustle in and take over, but they want a relationship and Tony may want to stir something up, but he won't!

OK, Ani Serena, it sounds like it would be ideal to have a covered area to keep the food dry from the rain and snow.

I'll have to see what I can do. We have a member who is very clever about buildings who could possibly help us. Maia, do you have any ideas on what it would look like?

Something with a roof and rather open is the idea. It could be a wall with food on one side or the other. Generally, when the coons are eating, the cats will pull back. But if it is just one coon and the cats, they could eat on each side of the wall. All the feeding could take place in one area, but there can be separation to make it accessible to all of them. Keep it open so no one feels trapped in any way. There could be a straight wall with some perpendicular divider walls separating the area into four feeding stations.

OK, I am beginning to see what you are talking about! Thank you so much—this is so wonderful!

You are so welcome, Ani Serena! Thank you for looking after our cats and coons! The cats and the coons have wisdom to share. They know you all get that. They asked me to thank you and all the members for being their guardians, and to also thank you for the honor of having the opportunity to share what they really wanted.

Thank you so much, Maia—you are so wonderful!

Less than a week after our call, I received a text with a photo of the new wall at the temple with four covered feeding stations. The cats and coons were doing great! Everyone was at peace and living in harmony.

CHAPTER TEN

Magic and Miracles

P ets are ingenious about finding creative ways to get their messages across to their people. Odd behaviors from them, and even appearing in their people's dreams, will often inspire the humans to arrange a conversation for their pet.

In some cases, a pet who I have talked with from a previous consultation will actually begin to show up in my own life. For instance, I recently began to have thoughts of a cat named Magic who I had met previously in telepathic communications on a number of occasions at the request of her person, a woman named Ava. It had been at least six months since our last meeting.

For a few days, she had been suddenly popping into my mind until I finally stopped to listen to what she wanted to share.

It was a Monday morning when the phone rang and I heard Ava's voice. I had left her a message earlier and she was curious to know why I was calling.

We were saying our hellos and catching up when Ava's curiosity got the best of her and she said:

Maia, why were you calling?

Ava, this is kind of unusual but Magic has been popping into my mind for a few days now and she says she has something she would like to share with you. That's why I am calling. Do you have a few minutes so I can share her message with you?

Yes, Maia! I would love to hear from her!

Magic had actually passed away a few years before I began to communicate with the cats Ava currently has, so I did not meet her during the time she was in her body, but she was a frequent presence, in spirit, in Ava's home. It was as if she still lived there, and was often in Ava's thoughts even though she no longer lived there in the physical sense.

It was unusual for Magic to make a particular request like this to talk with us, but it was not unusual for her to periodically interrupt the other cats when they were talking with me to share her opinion on something of importance to her.

Now that both Ava and I were available to listen, Magic was ready to begin talking.

Ava eagerly waited for a few moments as I listened to Magic and asked her some questions to be sure I was clear on the details about what she was expressing.

Let me pause here for a few moments to say something about Ava and her life so that you will get the full effect of Magic's unusual request. Ava is an extraordinary woman of many life experiences, travels and ease in different cultures and was experiencing some rather serious health challenges which limited her mobility and freedom. The limitations to her mobility were upsetting to her and she wanted nothing more than to regain her health and, with that, her freedom.

Now she did not dare dream of travel or adventure like she had experienced in the past, when she could barely move about the house.

When I got clear about what Magic wanted to request of Ava, I didn't see how it could be possible and thought it might even be upsetting for Ava to hear. But I was committed to sharing the cat's truth so I asked her:

Magic, why do you want to share this? Will it upset your woman to hear this?

Magic quickly replied:

I understand your concern. I want to share this because it will actually give my Woman a lift in her spirits, and you and she will be amazed at what is possible.

OK, thank you, Magic! I will share it!

I paused for a moment trying to think of a gentle way to share Magic's request, but ended up simply blurting it out.

Ava, Magic wants you to take a trip to Egypt. She wants you to first simply imagine it and allow yourself to consider it.

Maia, you know I would love to go to Egypt but I am not feeling well enough; I cannot really get around. I don't think I can consider this right now.

I understand, Ava! I get it. Let me be with Magic for another moment and see if she is really serious about this.

Magic, are you really serious about this? Do you really think it would be good for her?

Of course!

And, then I heard other familiar voices. First, it was Ava's cat Chelsea saying:

Magic, I agree! I want her to go to Egypt!

Then Ava's cat Scamper chimed in: *I do too!*

All of the cats excitedly expressed their desire for Ava to travel to Egypt.

Ava, not only does Magic want you to go on this trip, but the other cats, Chelsea and Scamper, do too! They are very excited about this!

Maia, I don't see this as being so easy or possible.

Ava, let me ask the cats for ways to make this a reality.

I took a moment to pose the question:

Cats, do you have some suggestions as to how Ava can actually travel to Egypt under her current circumstances?

We do! She really can do this! And taking this trip will be so satisfying and nurturing. She has dreamed of this for years and it is important for her to have this experience—it will help her heal!

If she will simply agree to consider it and choose a possible date, she will begin to see herself healing to the extent that she feels comfortable making the journey. For our Woman to go to Egypt will be in some senses like going home to some ancient roots. When she returns, she will have a new sense of confidence and ease.

OK, I will share what you have said and suggest that she at

least consider it.

Thank you!

Ava, the cats simply want you to agree that you will consider making this trip. They say once you begin to consider it, you will begin to think about when you would go, who you would visit there and even what you will need to do to prepare for the trip. They want you to imagine it, and consider it. That's all they ask! Ava, will you agree to this?

Maia, I still don't see how it is possible right now but sure, I will consider it. Thinking about it will be fun. I have been dreaming of a taking a trip there ever since my husband passed away. Please thank the cats for talking with us and for their concern for me. I will consider it.

I will tell them Ava!

With Ava's last remarks, the cats were ecstatic!

It was about three weeks later when Ava and I talked again. The first thing she mentioned was the trip to Egypt. I could tell it had been on her mind a lot since we last talked. She let me know that although she had been considering it as the cats had requested, she still did not see it as being a possibility. She proceeded to remind me of the details of the health challenges she was facing, and of her concerns.

I simply listened and let her know that I understood. I continued to remind her of the word 'consider' that seemed to really stand out in the cats' request.

The next time I talked with Ava, she excitedly shared with

me that she had hired a coach to work with her to build up her strength. She was doing exercises while seated and already feeling stronger. She had also looked into traveling in the fall, which would be a great time for her to be in Egypt. And she had even communicated with a few of her relatives and friends there about the possibility. Everyone was very excited with the thought of seeing her.

Throughout the next four months, Ava and I talked; especially when she was up against something she wasn't sure how to deal with. I always suggested that we talk with the cats. They were so aligned with her concerning the importance of making the trip, and they always had some encouragement and insight that seemed to instantly ground her and stabilize her on her path.

One time we talked about her ability to get around during her travels and how she could actually manage all the flight connections. The cats had brought up the possibility of Ava asking her son to make the trip with her and they shared with us that there was something important for him about making this trip as well. But Ava was concerned that he would say no, or even worse that he would say yes and then change his mind at the last minute and not show up. From her past experience she did not trust him, and the thought of planning something with him and relying on him stressed her even in theory.

However, the cats continued to encourage Ava to talk with her son and even how to go about having a conversation with him about making the trip.

By the time we talked again a few weeks later, Ava was ready to purchase tickets for the flights and her son had agreed to go. He was actually very excited about the trip as well, and the two of them began a new conversation in their life, celebrating some things they had forgotten they had in common.

Ava was ecstatic and she sounded so alive!

Ava! You sound so happy!

I am! I can hardly believe it! I thought I would have to wait for a long time to go on a trip like this. To be honest with you, I thought I would probably never go to Egypt again with all I have been facing. I have been talking with my doctor ever since Magic asked to talk about this trip and asked me to consider it. My doctor was amazingly calm about the idea and he actually gave me permission to travel yesterday. I am thrilled to have his support! So what seemed impossible and not even worth considering is now a reality. I am leaving in three short weeks and have a lot of little things to do, but for the most part I am ready. I am also healing and feeling really good!

That is so great, Ava! I want to acknowledge you for really listening to the cats, and even when it seemed totally ridiculous to consider, you made a commitment to follow through with their request. Not only did you follow through with their request to simply consider the possibility, you actually have taken all the steps and more to make this dream a reality! I am very excited for you, and the cats are out-of-this-world happy about you having this opportunity.

I talked with Ava one last time before she departed on her adventure. Our conversation was with the cats to ask them their preferences and take any final requests from them for their care while she was away.

Ava called me a few days after settling back in after her trip. Her travels were miraculously simple. She experienced ease in getting around and joy in long-awaited visits with family and friends. She had created new memories with her son and they enjoyed the opportunity to spend more time together than she had since he was a boy. The photo she emailed me of the two of them said it all!

Whenever I talk with Ava now, we still marvel at this miraculous journey brought to us by Magic, and inspired by her cats Chelsea and Scamper!

One thing I have learned for sure in my conversations with animals is that what I or another human may see as the limit to what's possible is not the same as what the animals see. They continually amaze me with their request to simply open our minds and hearts. And when our minds and hearts are open, a whole new adventure begins—beyond what we can even imagine is possible!

NEW BOOKS NOW AVAILABLE!

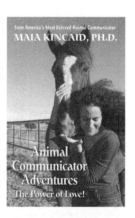
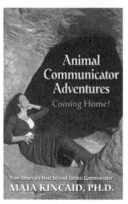

You have the natural ability to hear the animals too!
For information on awakening your natural abilities to listen
to animals and other wise beings of Nature contact:

Maia Kincaid Ph.D.
The Sedona International School for
Telepathic Animal & Nature Communication
Animal Communication University
www.maiakincaid.com

P.O. Box 4761
Sedona, AZ 86340
928-282-2604
All of Maia's books available through:
www.maiakincaid.com

Made in the USA
Middletown, DE
01 September 2020